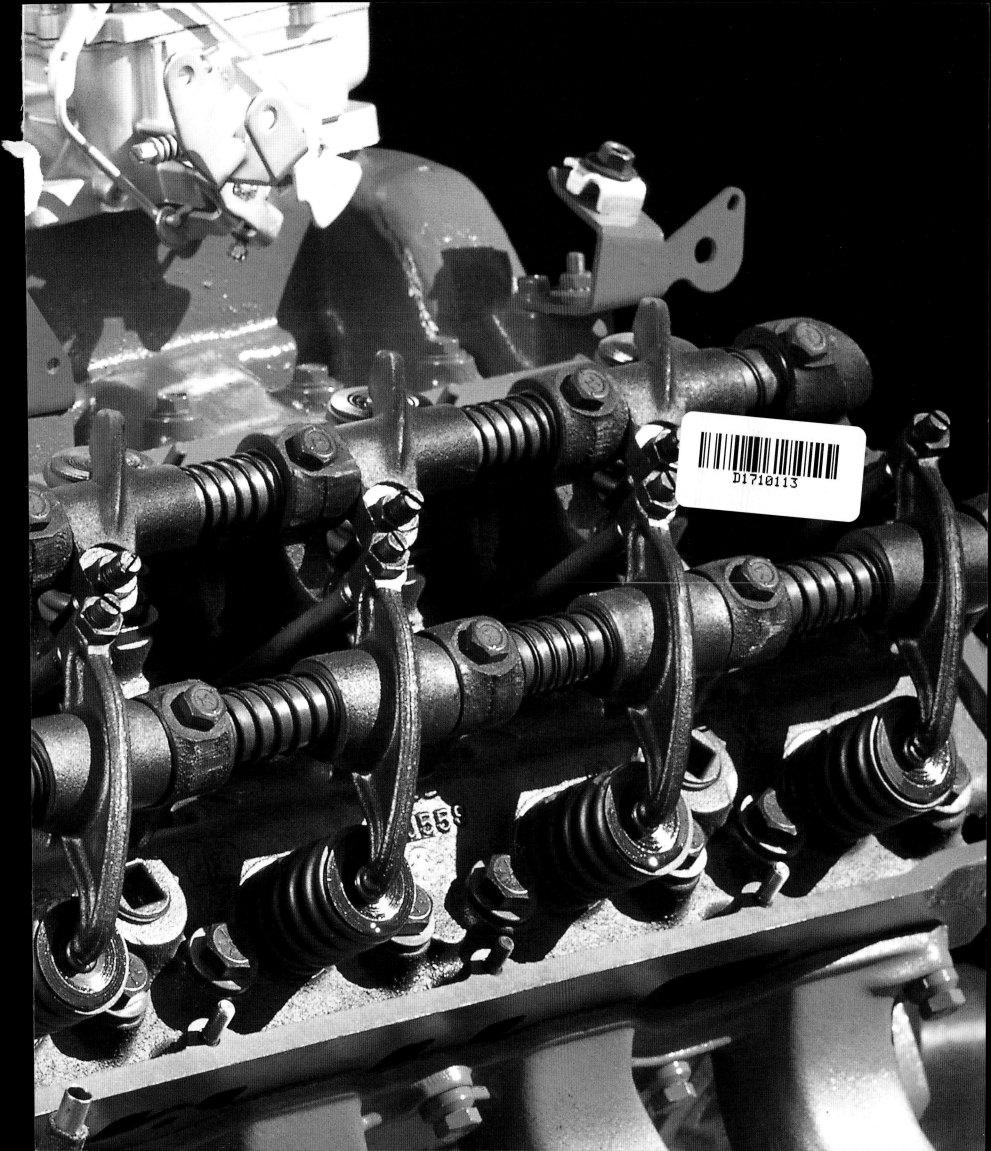

HEMI
MUSCLE CARS

DARWIN HOLMSTROM
PHOTOGRAPHY BY DAVID NEWHARDT

CRESTLINE

ACKNOWLEDGMENTS

While there are only two names on the front of this book, this tome wouldn't have become a reality without the help of scores of people. To everyone who put up with my demands for "just one more:" Thank You! Car people are the best!!

In no particular order: Erik Baltzar, Norman Weinfeld, Ferrell Davis, Bill Wieman, Dick Romm, Bill & Wanda Goldberg, Monty Bernstein, Steven Juliano, John Lazenby (!), Shannon A. Schilling, Sean Machado, Kenn Funk, Rick Gillespie, Steve Atwell Jr., Larry Zappone, Norm Kraus, Larry Weiner, Martin Swig, David Swig, Bruce Meyer, Byron Richardson, Robert Genat, David Christenholz, Ian Smale, Scott Brown from Chrysler Communications, Phyllis McClintock from Chrysler Corporate Historical Collection, the entire crew at Event Solutions International, Chief Operating Officer Bob DeFazio and Director of Operations Bob Klein from Toyota Speedway at Irwindale, the Walter P. Chrysler Museum, and Jill Painter from Mopars at the Strip.

A special thank you to my wife, Susan Foxx-Newhardt, who held down the fort while I was a professional tumbleweed, chasing Hemis from coast to coast.

I dedicate this book to my sons, Branden and Ryan.

—David Newhardt
Pasadena, California
2008

In addition to all of the above people David mentioned, without whom this or any other car book would not happen, I would like to thank my wife, Patricia, and all the Mopar people who indoctrinated me into their twisted cult during my formative years. I'd like to dedicate this book to my grandchildren, Jacob and Alison.

—Darwin Holmstrom
Maple Grove, MN
2008

This edition published in 2011 by
CRESTLINE
a division of BOOK SALES, INC.
276 Fifth Avenue Suite 206
New York, New York 10001
USA

This edition published by arrangement with Motorbooks, an imprint of MBI Publishing Company.

First published in 2008 by Motorbooks, an imprint of MBI Publishing Company, 400 First Avenue North, Suite 300, Minneapolis, MN 55401 USA

Library of Congress Cataloging-in-Publications Data

Holmstrom, Darwin.
  Hemi muscle cars / Darwin Holmstrom ; Photography by David Newhardt.
     p. cm.
  Includes index.
  ISBN-13: 978-0-7858-2783-2
  1. Chrysler automobile—History. 2. Chrysler automobile—Motors—History. 3. Muscle cars—United States—History. I. Newhardt, David, 1955- II. Title.
  TL215.C55H595 2008
  629.25'04--dc22
                                                              2008012314

On the cover: David Freers Photography, LLC.

On the endpapers: The legendary 426 Hemi in a revealing state of undress.

On the frontispiece: While there are no official records to prove it, the number of racers who backed down from a fight when they saw 426 HEMI on the opposing hood must surely be high.

On the title pages: The power of a Hemi engine could turn even the hardest tires into screaming, smoking victims.

Editor: Jeffrey Zuehlke
Designer: Mandy Iverson
Jacket Design: Simon Larkin

Printed in China

CONTENTS

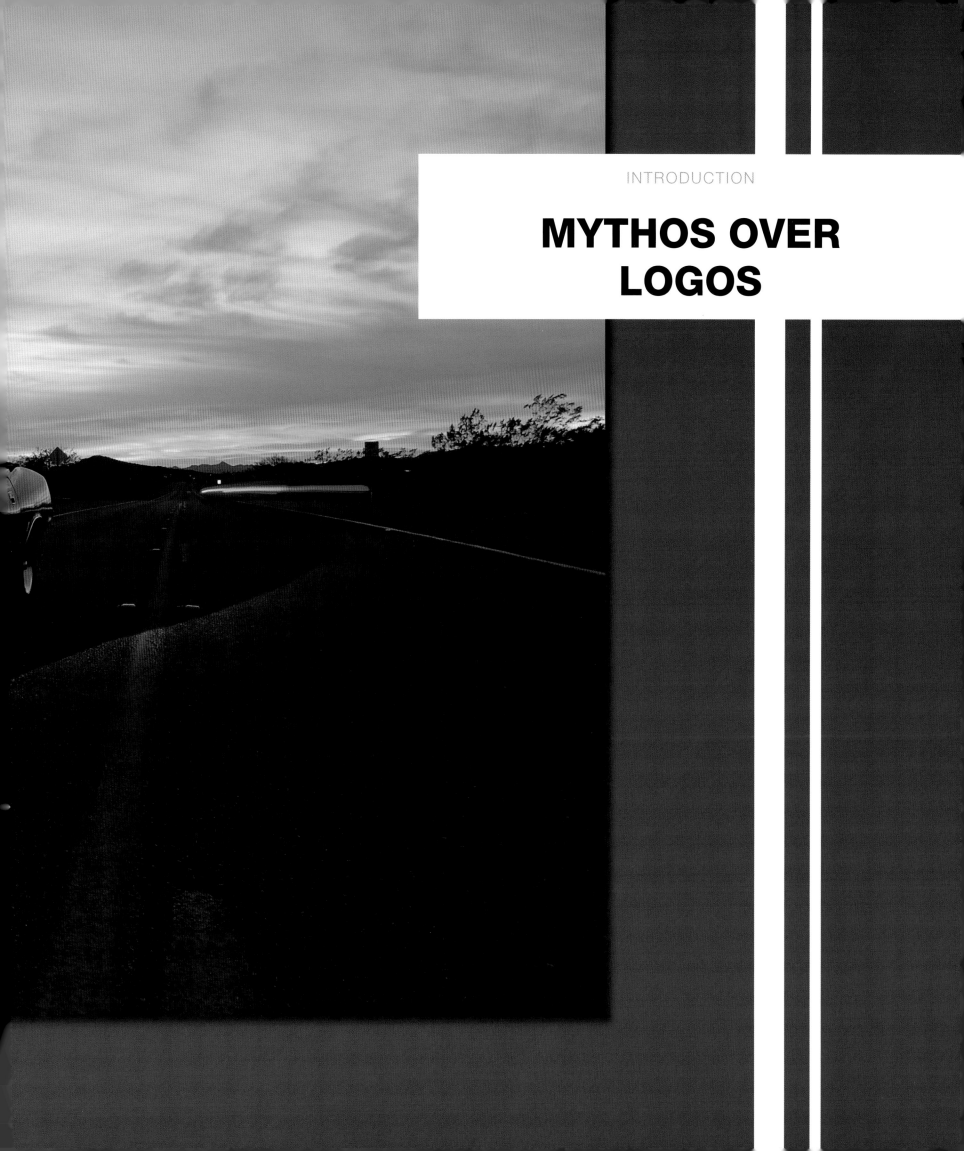

MYTHOS OVER LOGOS

MYTHOS OVER LOGOS

The German philosopher Martin Heidegger theorized that in the hierarchy of human thought, the mythological—mythos—takes precedence over the logical—logos. Heidegger defined logos as the sum of all current knowledge, and mythos as all the ideas and theories that had been discarded along the way to reaching that level of knowledge. Even though the logos virtually always superseded the mythos in practical application, Heidegger believed that the human animal, being more comfortable with the familiar and resistant to change, would pick mythos over logos when given the choice. The story of Chrysler's Hemi engine indicates that perhaps Heidegger was correct.

The Hemi holds a unique position in automotive history; it is the only technology that has transcended logos to become mythos. Humans can become mythologized. Some people possess mythic athletic abilities, others can drive a

Page 6-7: Looking like a hungry shark following the scent of blood, a 1970 Hemi 'Cuda prowls the night for prey.

Page 7-8: (Main) Beneath the radical shaker hood scoop of this 1971 'Cuda convertible resides one of the last 426 Hemi street engines Chrysler ever built. *(Inset)* In 1970 and 1971 Chrysler offered the Hemi engine in its E-body pony cars, the Plymouth 'Cuda and Dodge Challenger. Shown are the very first and very last convertible Hemi 'Cudas ever built, the red 1970 being the first and the white 1971 being the last.

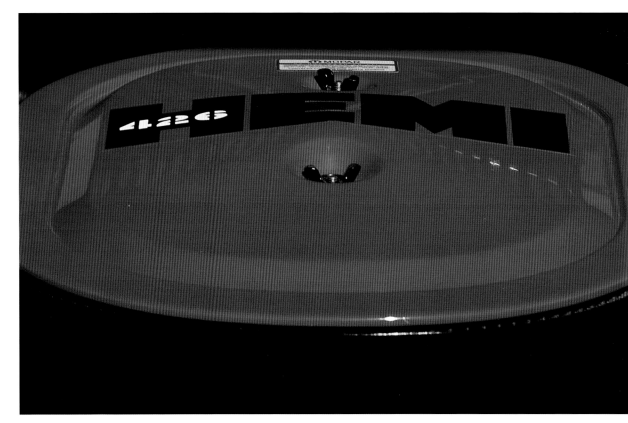

The heart of Hemi mythology is the mighty V-8 engine with hemispherical combustion chambers.

car or ride a motorcycle as if they were superhuman, while still others become legends through great accomplishments, such as inventing a cure for a disease, leading people through times of great distress, or besting all competition in any field. And some people become legends simply by inspiring other people.

Similarly, machines can achieve mythic status. An individual machine can attain wide recognition. For example, Charles Lindbergh's *Spirit of St. Louis* is as famous as its celebrated pilot. A manufacturer can likewise attain mythic status if it dominates a certain market niche. Any model of Ferrari conjures the image of a mythic sports or grand touring car. It doesn't matter the model; if it's a Ferrari, it's an icon. Even a manufacturer known for building pedestrian transportation devices can create a legendary model, as Ford did when it created the Mustang.

But rarely does a technology become mythological. Perhaps this is because by its very nature technology is part of the logos—it is, in fact, the very face with which logos presents itself to the world—and logos is the antithesis of mythos.

Yet this unlikely scenario is exactly what happened with Chrysler's Hemi engine. Chrysler adopted hemispherical-head technology in an attempt to build an efficient V-8 engine that could compete with the overhead valve V-8 engines being produced by Oldsmobile and Cadillac. The unintended byproduct of this effort was the creation of one of the most dominant engine designs ever unleashed on public highways.

Any argument about whose car was the fastest usually ended when someone dropped the name "Hemi."

In the Hemi production engine Chrysler created an automotive icon to rival the most exclusive European sports car brands. Shown is a 341-cubic-inch, 320 horsepower De Soto Fire Flite from a 1956 Adventurer. *Larry Zappone*

No other engine ever produced by an American automobile manufacturer had the sheer visual impact of a 426 Hemi.

The race Hemi engines can be distinguished by their chrome valve covers (the street Hemis had a black-wrinkle finish), and by the arrangement of their two gigantic four-barrel carburetors. The street Hemis featured their carbs mounted in line, while the race Hemis used cross-ram manifolds that located the carbs diagonally between the cylinder heads. *David Gooley*

WHAT IS A HEMI?

A hemispherical combustion chamber is simply a dome-shaped combustion chamber. This design has inherent advantages. A dome-shaped combustion chamber with a centrally located spark plug allows the fuel charge to burn evenly. The flame starts at the center of the combustion chamber and pushes down on the piston with even pressure. It also allows for the use of two very large valves. (Technically, when a dome-shaped combustion chamber uses three or more valves, it is called a "pent-roof" design.)

The hemi design also brings with it certain disadvantages. For example, a dome-shaped combustion chamber splays the intake and exhaust valves out at a less-than-ideal angle—Chrysler's original Hemi had a valve angle of 58.5 degrees. This forced the use of wide, heavy heads topped by complicated and heavy rocker arms that limited ultimate engine rpm. Thus, hemispherical heads work best on large, torque-laden, low-revving engines that don't rely on ultra-high-rpm power and aren't penalized as much as smaller engines for excessive weight.

This made the hemi an ideal design for the big pushrod V-8s powering American performance cars, engines that emphasize low-end torque over peak horsepower output. But the hemi is not unique to American muscle. In fact, U.S. manufacturers were among the last to take advantage of the design. Since the earliest years of the twentieth century, European automobiles with domed combustion chambers had been winning races around the world. Peugeot began

In 1968 Chrysler manufactured a small run of Hemi-powered A-body cars for drag racing. Chrysler built 70 Hemi Barracudas *(shown)* and 80 Hemi Darts. *David Gooley*

using race engines with pent-roof combustion chambers in 1912. Jaguar and BMW produced passenger cars with hemispherical combustion chambers before Chrysler introduced its first Hemi-powered production car.

Chrysler wasn't even the first U.S. automaker to produce engines with domed combustion chambers. Companies such as Duesenberg and Stutz had produced such cars long before Chrysler began developing its production Hemi. The Welch Tourist, first shown at the Chicago

The Hemi-powered A-bodies came in unpainted (body-in-white) form; since these were built for the track instead of the street, owners were required to paint the cars in their own personal racing colors.

Automobile Salon in 1903, featured a 20-horsepower two-cylinder engine with hemispherical combustion chambers. This car, built by the Chelsea Manufacturing Company, a bicycle-manufacturing operation run by the Welch brothers in Chelsea, Michigan, is likely the earliest production car to use a hemi engine, beating Chrysler to the market by nearly half a century. In 1904 the brothers moved their operation to Pontiac, Michigan, where they further developed the hemi engine design. They built a four-cylinder version, and then a six-cylinder version, but hemi development ceased shortly after General Motors purchased Chelsea in 1909. Apparently GM saw no reason to continue developing the hemi engine.

RACE ON SUNDAY, MYTHOLOGIZE ON MONDAY

No one doubts that the hemispherical combustion chamber is an excellent design, but that still doesn't explain how Chrysler managed to elevate to the realm of myth a technology that was nearly as old as the internal combustion engine itself. Chrysler certainly did not set out to create an automotive icon with its Hemi. In fact, while the engine was in production, Chrysler never referred to its original domed-combustion-chamber engine as a "hemi." Internally, Chrysler called it "the double-rocker engine," referring to its complex valvetrain mechanism, and gave it the marketing name "FirePower." The firm would not officially give the engine the proper name "Hemi" until the advent of the second-generation engines in the early 1960s. Eventually Chrysler would go on to trademark the term, spelling it with a capital "H" from that point on. (For the sake of clarity, we're using the capital "H" whenever we use "Hemi" as a proper noun for a Chrysler engine in this book.)

At first, Chrysler's marketing types didn't realize what an automotive icon the company had created with its hemispherical engine design; the first generation of engines weren't even called "Hemis"—instead the company gave them the marketing name "FirePower."

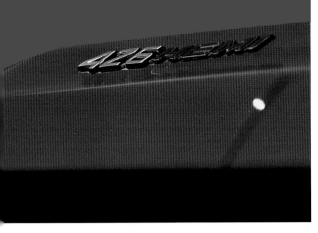

By the time Chrysler introduced the second-generation Hemis in the 1960s, it acknowledged the fact that everyone called the cars "Hemis" and did the same.

Racing played an enormous part in elevating the Hemi to mythic status. Hemi-powered cars began winning races almost as soon as buyers could get them out on the dirt tracks that are found in nearly every county fairground in America. It was on a Detroit, Michigan, fairground track in August 12, 1951, that Howard W. "Tommy" Thompson took the first of what would become many National Association for Stock Car Auto Racing (NASCAR) checkered flags earned by Hemi-powered cars. In the years that followed, sports car builder Briggs Cunningham would turn in impressive performances at Le Mans with his Hemi-powered specials, and Lee Petty won NASCAR's Grand National championship in 1954 in a Hemi-powered Chrysler.

Chrysler Hemis have dominated the sport of drag racing since Don Garlits decided to make a practice run in his Hemi-powered tow car back in the mid-1950s. Since then, most of the fabled race teams like Sox & Martin have been winning races with Hemi-powered cars.

Not long after that, Don Garlits bought a Hemi engine from a junkyard, installed it in his dragster, and made the Hemi the dominant force in American drag racing.

Racing would go on to play an even larger role in the legend of the Hemi during the design's second incarnation in the 1960s, but the rise of the technology to mythological status involved a lot more than just success in competition. After all, Hudson's Hornet dominated NASCAR racing in the early part of the 1950s, yet no one ever considered its side-valve inline six mythological. Clearly, there's more to the ascendance of the Hemi than simple race-on-Sunday-sell-on-Monday marketing hype.

THE RIGHT ENGINE IN THE RIGHT CAR AT THE RIGHT TIME

Part of the engine's appeal had to do with the era in which it existed. Throughout the 1950s the company's overhead-valve V-8 engines consistently produced more power than anything offered by the competition. Anyone marketing the baddest cars built in the United States was certain to make a powerful impression on the brains of 70 million baby boomers as they entered puberty. This was the generation that was obsessed with cars like no other generation before or since. In his book *Lake Wobegon Days,* author Garrison Keillor wrote that the Lutherans in his hometown drove Fords because the Ford dealer was Lutheran, and the Catholics drove Chevrolets because the Chevrolet dealer was Catholic. Or perhaps it was vice versa. Either way, it didn't really matter; if you were a Mopar guy and you lusted after those Hemi-powered bad boys, you were going to hell anyway.

As has always been the case, young males in the hormonal throes of puberty found hell and fast cars a lot more interesting than heaven and slow cars. Thus the Chrysler Hemis

Whether on the track or on the street, Hemi-powered cars have always excelled at leaving big, tire-smoking impressions on passers-by.

In an era when any overhead-valve V-8 was an impressive piece of machinery, the big, dual-quad Hemis of the 1950s proved more impressive than any other American engine. *Larry Zappone*

With its dual four-barrel carburetors, high-end components, and extensive hand assembly, the Hemi was a prohibitively expensive engine to build.

U.S. soldiers stationed in Vietnam lusted over the Hemi ads of the 1960s as much as they lusted over the latest centerfolds in *Playboy* magazine. *David Newhardt Collection*

became permanently imprinted in tens of millions of adolescent brains. David Grovum, a hot rodder from Grygla, Minnesota, recalls the impression the Hemi made on him when he was a preteen: "The old 392s were extremely vicious cars. An old guy who worked in the creamery in my hometown had a 392 with two four-barrels. I don't know if he ever raced it, but he must have worn out the hood hinges showing off the engine. It was an impressive-looking piece of machinery."

A decade later, when millions of baby boomers found themselves torn away from their hometowns to be sent to the jungles of Vietnam, the national zeitgeist played an even more important role in mythologizing the Hemi. Grovum was one such young man, whose budding love affair with American performance cars was interrupted by an Uncle Sam-sponsored overseas excursion. "You got some guy laying up in a hooch in Southeast

Hemis dominated all forms of racing in the United States, but none more completely than drag racing.

Asia," Grovum says, "reading those Mopar ads, seeing those quarter-mile times, he's going to want one of those cars when he comes home."

Colin Comer, one of the world's foremost muscle-car experts and founder of Colin's Classic Cars, an exotic car dealership in Milwaukee, Wisconsin, attributes part of the iconic status of the Hemi engine to its exclusivity. "It was an astronomically expensive engine to build," Comer says, referring to the 426-cubic-inch Hemi (though the original Hemi of the 1950s was also prohibitively expensive to produce). Even though checking the Hemi option on the order

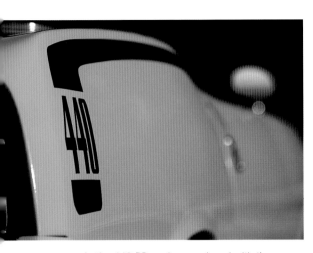

In the 440 RB engines equipped with three two-barrel carburetors the Hemi had real competition. In 1969 the 440-6-Pack/440-6-BBL cars equaled the torque output of the Hemis, at least on paper.

While the spec sheets would seem to indicate that the 440-6 cars would have roughly the same performance as a Hemi car, in reality the 440-6 cars outperformed the Hemi cars in the quarter mile, at least in stock form.

sheet could increase the price of a car by up to 50 percent, the Hemi of the 1960s was a loss-leader for Chrysler—it cost the company more to build the engines than it charged customers to buy them, and the company lost money producing the 426 Hemis. But profit wasn't the point of the 426 street Hemi; Chrysler only sold the engines to customers in order to qualify them for various forms of racing.

The prices Chrysler charged for street Hemis helped elevate the engine to a mythological status. "You pay $830 for an engine option, you expect it to be fast," Comer says. "A 440 Six Pack was a lot better motor out of the box—it would easily run with a Hemi, and it cost $500 less. That would buy a lot of gas, but if a guy is intent on buying the fastest car a dealer offers and he sees that one engine costs $500 more than another, he naturally assumes the more expensive engine has to be faster."

"A CASTRATED BULL"

In the reality of the American stoplight drag race (as opposed to the reality of the spec sheet in a car magazine), a strong-running 440 would outrun a bone-stock Hemi, at least in the quarter-mile. "You didn't want to race a Hemi past a quarter-mile," David Grovum says. To buy a Hemi in the 1960s required real commitment; it required an initial financial commitment, and it required commitment on the part of the owner to spend the money and do the finishing work required to bring the engine to its full potential.

Craig Buness, a hot rodder from Crookston, Minnesota, says, "The street Hemi had the most potential of any engine ever sold to the public. But as they came from the factory, they were castrated bulls. The Hemis were basically unfinished race engines. Hemis were select-fit

Each of the original 426 race Hemis was extensively tested at Chrysler's Highland Park engine lab. In many respects, these were hand-assembled engines.

Sometimes the myth of the Hemi didn't match the reality, at least until the Hemi had been tuned by someone who knew how to extract the mighty engine's untapped potential.

Norma "Mr. Norm" Kraus's Grand Spaulding Dodge in Chicago, Illinois, was ground zero for Mopar performance. *David Newhardt Collection*

engines, because Chrysler knew how owners were going to use them. All production motors have tolerance variations—you can get a real loose one or a real tight one. A special low-production engine like a Hemi has minimal variation. An engine like that will burn some oil, but it will be the best raw material available for building a race engine."

The problem was converting that raw material into a usable engine. "Your average mechanic at a Chrysler dealership," Buness continues, "he knew how to rebuild a slant-six. He didn't know anything about dual-carb, solid-lifter Hemis. A dealer mechanic would do more harm than good working on a high-performance engine like that."

Even specialty shops sometimes had a hard time coaxing performance out of a Hemi. Buness tells of Glen Myrold, a drag racer from Rolle, North Dakota, who raced a Hemi: "He bought a yellow-and-black Super Bee. He heard Mr. Norm's ad on the radio: 'You getting your ass handed to you? Come on down to Grand Spaulding and see Mr. Norm. Make sure you ask for the 4.10

Unlike the factory Hemi A-body cars, which were built to dominate drag racing, Bob Riggle built his infamous *Hemi under Glass* Barracuda to perform wheelie exhibitions.

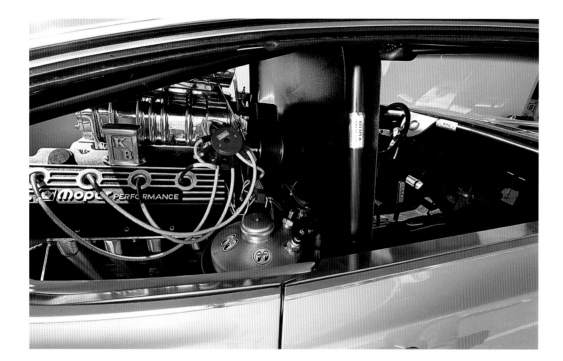

rear end.' Glen went to Chicago and said, 'I'm getting beat by 396 Chevelles. What do I have to do?' He had his car dyno tuned, put on a set of headers, put in 4.10 gears, and came back to town thinking he'd have the fastest car around. And he got beat. It was embarrassing."

Myrold's experience was fairly typical, but that was by design. Larry Ohren, owner of Pennington County Performance, a shop in Thief River Falls, Minnesota, that specializes in Mopar restoration and customization, says, "Chrysler didn't care if the engines underperformed as delivered, because most of the people buying them shouldn't have been buying them in the first place. The people who needed to know how to make a Hemi perform knew how to make a Hemi perform."

PRESENCE

Given all the challenges and expense involved with owning and racing a Hemi, it's amazing that the engine enjoyed any popularity at all, much less that it became an automotive icon. An exorbitant retail price, success in the hands of professional race teams, and untapped performance potential can't completely explain the rise of the Hemi into the realm of the mythological.

Colin Comer believes that the engine itself is the final component of the Hemi's rise to mythic status. "The engine has presence," Comer says. "It has visual impact. You open the hood, it's all motor. It has the perception of speed. You look at it and think, 'That's why this fucker costs $830.'"

This is, of course, not very logical. But as old Marty Heidegger pointed out, mythos trumps logos every time. ■

"THE HOT ROD BOYS"

CHAPTER ONE

"THE HOT ROD BOYS"

By the time Chrysler introduced its first passenger cars with V-8 engines, the company's engineers already knew a thing or two about hemispherical combustion chambers. They began experimenting with hemispherical heads on the company's six-cylinder engines almost as soon as Walter P. Chrysler founded the company in the 1920s. This work eventually led to the Hemi-6 series, a family of six-cylinder engines produced by Chrysler Australia.

During World War II (1939–1945) Chrysler developed a V-16 aircraft engine with hemispherical combustion chambers. Conservatively rated at 2,500 horsepower, the engine produced well over 3,000 horsepower—enough to propel a P-47 Thunderbolt fighter to a speed of 504 miles per hour at 15,000 feet. The powerplant showed great promise, but only a few test units were built before the war ended and development money dried up.

Page 26-27: In the 1951 running of the Carrera Panamericana, Bill Sterling drove a nearly stock 1951 Saratoga Club Coupe to a first-in-class finish, and finished third overall.

Page 28-29: (Main) The then-new Hemi engine made the 1951 Chryslers competitive in all forms of automobile racing. It was practically race-ready right out of the box.

(Inset) Accomplished racer John Fitch drove this 1951 Saratoga Club Coupe in that year's Carrera Panamericana road race across Mexico.

Chrysler wasn't the only company to experiment with hemi heads in the mid-1940s. During the war, Ford shipped a bunch of trucks to England with engines that were so weak "they wouldn't pull a sick whore out of church," according to David Grovum. Ford contracted a brilliant young engineer named Zora Arkus-Duntov to develop an overhead valve conversion kit for the side-valve engines used in the trucks. Arkus-Duntov and his brother Yura Arkus-Duntov designed a set of aluminum heads with hemispherical combustion chambers. The war had ended by the time the Arkus-Duntov brothers had the heads ready for use, so they lost their military market and instead sold the heads to the budding hot-rod market under the brand-name "Ardun." Because of the relatively crude state of metallurgy at the time, these heads suffered from problems caused by different metals expanding at different rates, but the performance of the overhead valve hemi heads showed the design had great promise.

Walter P. Chrysler. *Copyright Chrysler LLC. Used with permission.*

OVERCOMING THE AIRFLOW

Chrysler had become an extremely conservative company following the spectacular failure of its Airflow automobiles of the 1930s. Walter Percy Chrysler had gambled everything on the radical Airflow design, introduced for the 1934 model year. When the car flopped, he nearly lost the company that bears his name.

Chrysler, a flamboyant character with a sharp tongue, a short temper, and a predilection for grandiosity, started life as a laborer on a farm and worked his way up the ladder to become the president of Buick. From there, he went on to form his eponymous automobile company, and by 1926 Chrysler Corporation was the third largest automobile manufacturer in America,

Zora Arkus-Duntov and his brother Yura developed a kit that converted the Ford flathead V-8 engine to an overhead valve configuration, improving volumetric efficiency. The Ardun head featured hemispherical combustion chambers.

The war ended before the Ardun heads were ready for production so the brothers marketed them to hot rodders.

The Airflow got its name from its advanced aero-dynamic shape. Its round contours and smooth lines were unlike anything seen on an automobile before.

behind only General Motors and Ford. Chrysler was justifiably a self-confident man. Hubris on W. P. Chrysler's part undoubtedly contributed to the disastrous decision to bet the future of his company on the Airflows, but the cars themselves had a lot to recommend them. The Airflows' designs had been ground-breaking, with such modern features as aerodynamic shapes formed in a wind tunnel, hydraulic brakes, and tubular-steel space frames covered with steel body panels. Unfortunately, the reliability of these advanced cars suffered because they had been rushed into production at the insistence of Chrysler himself, a decision that diminished any notion of his own infallibility. Between spotty quality control and a shocking design that failed to find acceptance

While the Airflow's profile doesn't seem that unusual today, when the design was introduced in 1934, the only way it could have been more shocking would have been if it could have flown.

in the marketplace, sales were dismal. The Airflow debacle sent Chrysler Corporation into an economic tailspin that would continue for several years after Walter Chrysler's death in 1940. Not until the immediate postwar years did the company finally recover.

Worse yet, this failure wasn't just disastrous for Chrysler Corporation's bottom line; it also demoralized the company's management. Fearful of a repeat of the Airflow catastrophe, Chrysler executives became extremely cautious and conservative.

The flathead sixes and eights powering the Airflow were the only engines available in Chrysler cars prior to the introduction of the original Hemi.

Chrysler was a high-end car company and the Airflow's luxurious interior rivaled that of any of its competitors.

The Airflow introduced such innovations as hydraulic brakes and a tubular-steel frame covered with steel body panels. Unfortunately the cars were rushed into production and quality suffered.

The man who succeeded Walter Chrysler in 1935 epitomized this risk-averse mindset. Kaufman Thuma (K.T.) Keller (1885–1966) may have learned the lessons of the Airflow too well: his adherence to time-tested automotive design would prove to be almost as financially disastrous as the Airflow experiment. Suffice to say, with Keller at the helm, the Chrysler Corporation of the 1940s was not an organization prone to taking risks.

Chrysler engineers used a wind tunnel to develop the Airflow's advanced shape. The result was a car that looked nothing like the square-cornered cars produced by Chrysler's competitors.

The Airflow proved to have too much innovation for the conservative car-buying public. The car failed to find an audience, sending Chrysler Corporation into an economic tailspin that nearly destroyed the company.

Keller may have resisted change in any form, but after the war even the most hidebound Chrysler executive knew the company needed something more than the antiquated side-valve inline sixes and eights that had powered the company's passenger cars up until that point. Styling hadn't changed after the war—like the other major U.S. automakers (with the notable exception of Studebaker), Chrysler continued to build the same basic cars it had built before the war with only minor styling tweaks, such as revised grilles and chrome ornamentation. The automakers used this quick and easy approach in an effort to amortize the costs of the dies and assembly lines that they had built earlier in the decade. They could get away with this because they were enjoying a kind of seller's market that had rarely, if ever, been seen before in history. From 1942 to 1945, the U.S. government had placed a ban on civilian car production. When the ban was finally lifted in late 1945, U.S. buyers were so hungry for new cars to replace their worn-out jalopies that they happily bought just about anything the automakers built.

Styles didn't change in the immediate postwar years, but the market did change. In fact, it exploded. Families were growing larger and more affluent, and they needed larger cars to transport the prodigious number of children they were creating in the aftermath of the war. Bigger cars needed more powerful engines, so Chrysler assigned an engine development team that included James Zeder, Ray White, Mel Carpentier, John Platner, and William Drinkard the task of developing a modern engine. Ev Moeller, one of the first people to graduate from the Chrysler Institute in 1939, joined the team in 1947. Moeller had worked in the aircraft engine development program during the war and was familiar with the potential of hemispherical combustion chambers.

In the years following the war, the team tested engines from around the world and found that a small four-cylinder engine built by the English manufacturer Healey had the best power-to-displacement ratio of any power plant they tested. The Healey featured two camshafts mounted high in the block, pushing short pushrods that operated pairs of valves opening into hemispherical combustion chambers. Testing conducted by John Platner showed that the hemi design had superior volumetric and thermal efficiency—that is, the domed shape of the combustion chamber maximized the thrusting force created by the combustion process while minimizing the loss of power through heat transference. This allowed the use of higher compression ratios without causing detonation, making the design far more efficient than the side-valve design used in Chrysler's production car engines. In a paper presented to the Society of Automotive Engineers in 1951, James Zeder wrote:

> Throughout all this test work, the hemispherical combustion chamber consistently developed the highest efficiency of all the many designs tested. In other words, this chamber was able to put to work more of the heat energy available in the fuel than could any other production passenger car engine in America. . . . Equally important to the high performance of the

Kaufman Thuma "K. T." Keller. *Copyright Chrysler LLC. Used with permission.*

FirePower engine is the exceptional breathing capacity of this hemispherical chamber design. The cross-section of a FirePower cylinder shows the many features that are conducive to high volumetric efficiency, or breathing. The valves are not crowded together, nor are they surrounded closely by combustion chamber walls. Both ports are ideally streamlined with a minimum of directional change. The complete separation of the ports, together with the wide space between the valve seats, assures that the incoming charge picks up a minimum of heat from the hot exhaust. In addition, the flow within the cylinder is not restricted by any barriers or tortuous passes.

The team first tested the hemi design on the A161, an in-line six engine that they modified to accept hemispherical heads. They used double overhead cams to operate the valves, which was standard practice on many of the high-performance hemi engines being built in Europe at the time. In testing, the engine ran smoothly and produced impressive power, even on the 80 octane pump gas commonly available at the time, but the wide angle of the valves required a complex, twin-chain cam drive. While this was a common design in Europe, the engineering team believed such a system was too maintenance-intensive for the average American car buyer, as well as too expensive to manufacture. They decided to pursue a different design.

CONFIGURATION WARS

The team knew that Cadillac and Oldsmobile were developing overhead valve (OHV) V-8 engines and they didn't want Chrysler to be caught with its corporate pants down, so team leader William Drinkard proposed that Chrysler build its own high-performance V-8s—V-8s with hemispherical combustion chambers. Drinkard's proposal hit Chrysler's headquarters in Highland Park, Michigan, like a Molotov cocktail. Chrysler Vice Chairman Fred Zeder, head of engine development (who also happened to be James Zeder's older brother), believed that there was no reason to deviate from the successful inline engine architecture that had served the company so well up until that point. As head of Chrysler's engine development since the formation of the company, the elder Zeder presented a formidable obstacle to making the Hemi V-8 engine a reality.

In 1948, after much corporate infighting that included a fair amount of bickering between the Zeder siblings, K.T. Keller ended all the arguments and gave the hemispherical-head V-8 project his blessing. Yet even without formal approval, Drinkard's team had been developing an

OHV V-8 engine on the sly since the war ended, continuing development work begun during the war. Within weeks they had the A182, a prototype 330-cubic-inch V-8 with hemispherical heads, running on a dynamometer.

The A182 produced impressive power, and Drinkard received permission to develop a production version. Mel Carpentier's team took the next step, building a production prototype of the Hemi engine, the A239. More compact than the A182 (even though displacement increased slightly to 331 cubic inches) the A239 was built with manufacturing considerations given the utmost priority.

Beyond power, the engineering team also emphasized durability in the new V-8. Drinkard insisted that the engine last at least 100,000 miles without needing to have major components such as pistons, rings, and bearings replaced. But despite such lofty goals, the A239 and subsequent prototype engines suffered from catastrophic camshaft failures. The profiles of the cam lobes loaded stress into the valves; when these loads were transferred back into the cam lobes, it caused the lobe surfaces to disintegrate.

The failures were a result of the team's inexperience in developing overhead valve engines. To solve the problem, Bob Rodger and a team of engineers worked long hours to develop a reliable camshaft. Rodger, the son of a New York dairy farming family, earned a master's degree from Chrysler's Institute of Engineering in 1941 and became the head of Chrysler division's engineering department in 1952. The fix involved using graphite-coated tappets and required developing an entirely new manufacturing process. Rodger's team also specified the use of additives in the engine oil to ensure camshaft reliability.

The location of the spark plugs also presented a challenge to the designers. While ideal for fast and efficient combustion, the centrally located spark plugs were difficult to access without removing valve covers. To resolve the issue, the engine design team ran steel tubes through the covers down to the spark plug ports. O-ring seals kept debris out of the cylinder heads and oil inside of them. Long ceramic boots covered the plugs, and the plug wires ran beneath a metal cover to the back of the engine. The result was a clean, purposeful-looking engine that appeared elegant and brutish at the same time. In addition to being the most powerful engine of its day, the new Hemi would also be the most handsome.

Given the performance potential of the engine, the engineering team specified heavy-duty parts throughout, such as shot-peened forged-steel crankshafts that spun in five main bearings. Since the engine was being developed for use in luxury sedans rather than high-performance sports cars, ease of maintenance took precedence over raw power. Thus the new engine used hydraulic lifters instead of solid units, lowering the rev limit of the engine, but in turn eliminating the need for periodic valve adjustments.

Chrysler teamed up with Carter to develop a two-barrel carburetor that featured an integral water jacket to prevent the carb from icing up in cold weather. To make the engine more user friendly, it also featured an automatic choke. A lot of spark would be needed to extract the potential power from the Hemi design, so the team specified a dual-breaker ignition system.

Chrysler debuted the production 331.1-cubic-inch Hemi V-8 in 1951. When fitted in the top-line New Yorker, it provided smooth acceleration that was superior to prior Chrysler eight-cylinder engines.

THE PROTO-MUSCLE CARS

After extensive dyno and road testing, the Hemi engine was production-ready for the 1951 model year. By that time, the OHV V-8 competition from Oldsmobile and Cadillac had been on the market for two years—Cadillac introduced its V-8 in October 1948 and Oldsmobile's Rocket V-8 followed its corporate cousin to the market one month later. By 1951 the GM V-8s had already developed a following—both on the country's racetracks and in the marketplace.

For the newcomer from Chrysler to win customers away from the General Motors divisions, the new Hemi had to be more than good; it had to be the best engine available in any American car dealership.

It was. The engine, given the marketing name "FirePower," featured a compression ratio of 7.5:1 and had a 1.81-inch intake valve and a 1.5-inch exhaust valve. It arrived at its 331.1-cubic-inch displacement through a cylinder bore of 3.8125 inches and a stroke of 3.625 inches. This made the engine an "oversquare" design (the bore was larger than the stroke). The primary advantage of such a design is a shorter stroke for a given displacement, resulting in slower piston speeds—a piston traveling up and down a 3.6-inch cylinder bore at 2,000 rpm is covering a lot less ground than a piston traveling at the same rate in a 4-inch cylinder bore. The end result is an engine that can run reliably at higher rpm, while at the same time extending the life of the engine by causing less wear and tear on the pistons, rings, rods, bearings, crankshaft, and cylinder bore at normal operating speeds.

Compared to the 330.0-cubic-inch Cadillac V-8 and 303.7-cubic-inch Olds Rocket engine, the new Hemi was remarkably efficient. The downside was that the Hemi heads were heavy; a pair weighed 120 pounds versus the 94-pound weight of a pair of Cadillac cylinder heads. Chrysler engineers compensated by keeping the weight of other components down, so both the Cadillac and Chrysler engines weighed about the same, around 700 pounds. Both engines used a 7.5:1 compression ratio, but the Hemi produced 180 horsepower, besting the Cadillac's 160 horsepower and the Olds' 135 horsepower by a good margin and proving the superiority of hemispherical combustion chambers when it came to producing raw horsepower. (Torque figures of the FirePower and Cadillac V-8 were identical, at 312 lb-ft apiece.)

This was years before the horsepower wars that took place a decade later; in 1951, 180 horsepower was an astounding number. It certainly made an impression on a young hot rodder from Florida named Donald Glenn Garlits. Recalling the first time he saw "180 horsepower" posted on a sign advertising the new Hemi in a Chrysler dealership window, the man who later became much better known as "Big Daddy" Don Garlits assumed that the dealer had made a mistake and had transposed the "8" and the "0." It seemed to him and his friends that "108 horsepower" was a lot more probable.

Exuding a patrician air, the 1951 Chrysler New Yorker was a desirable American luxury vehicle. The two-door coupe started at $3,348.

Though radical new technology resided under the hood, the basic New Yorker design was carried over for 1951. The big luxury car tipped the scales at 4,260 pounds, yet rode like a cloud.

Chrysler placed these large "V" hood ornaments on all of its V-8-equipped cars. The ornament was an art deco design originally seen on pre-war Chryslers.

The 1951 New Yorker's bench seats comfortably fit three average-sized adults. As befitting any top-of-the-line vehicle, the New Yorker's interior materials were of superior quality, and fit and finish were above reproach.

Chrysler made the FirePower standard equipment on the New Yorker and Imperial models, and offered it as an extra cost option on the Saratoga. The Windsor model soldiered on with the old in-line side-valve engines. With their new Hemi engines, these were the fastest luxury cars on the market, but none of them competed directly with the Rocket 88, which Oldsmobile had created by mounting its Rocket V-8 in its lighter 88 chassis. The Rocket 88 was the proto muscle car. So in July 1951, Chrysler responded by introducing a model that would take full advantage of the new Hemi engine: the Saratoga Club Coupe. Rather than a two-door version of the heavy Saratoga sedan, the Club Coupe used the lighter Windsor chassis, following Oldsmobile's lead with the Rocket 88. Chrysler might have been following Oldsmobile's lead by putting its hottest engine in its lightest chassis, but out on the street the 180-horsepower Club Coupe smoked the 135-horsepower Rocket 88.

Chrysler mated the 331 Hemi to a Fluid-Torque Drive semi-automatic transmission. This two-speed tranny had been in use for a number of years, and though it used a clutch on take-off, from there the driver simply had to momentarily lift the throttle to allow the transmission to shift to the next gear.

A New Yorker paced the Indianapolis 500 race in 1951, giving the new powerplant exposure in front of thousands of performance enthusiasts.

Postwar luxury cars were expected to carry at least four adults and their luggage, and the 1951 New Yorker was no exception. The rounded lines were in keeping with the styling direction of the era, a gentle evolution of prewar designs.

In 1951, an affluent businessman could step out of his personal airplane and into his Hemi-powered luxury car. Unlike later in the decade, the use of chrome trim was subdued and tasteful.

"A MAJOR STEP AHEAD IN AMERICAN AUTOMOTIVE HISTORY"

Once bolted into a midsized chassis, the superiority of the Hemi quickly made itself known on the street. When *Road & Track* magazine tested a Saratoga Club Coupe with a FirePower Hemi mounted in its engine bay for its November 1951 issue, the magazine got the car from 0 to 60 miles per hour in 10 seconds flat. The Cadillac Coupe DeVille took 13.5 seconds to get to 60; the Oldsmobile Rocket 88 took 12.5 seconds to accomplish the same. The magazine described the testing procedure it used to achieve its impressive results:

Internal combustion engines powered both of these transportation conveyances, yet while this aircraft embraced pre-war technology, the sturdy Chrysler used a cutting-edge powerplant.

By 1951 Chrysler sheetmetal had begun to look dated. Meanwhile, the company's competitors were already moving on to more modern designs.

With the selector in low range the clutch was disengaged and the engine revved to about 25 percent throttle (normal starts do not require use of clutch). . . . Depressing the throttle any more than 25 percent made the Chrysler sit still and peel rubber, losing precious split seconds. . . . Then with the engine winding to the proper point, the clutch was sharply engaged. At about 35 mph the clutch was again floored, and the throttle was held "full on." This put the 3rd gear into play and at around 65 mph the throttle was again backed off to allow the car to drop to 4th. When this is performed in proper sequence a 0-60 time of 10 seconds should result.

Road & Track, a magazine that has always favored European sporting hardware over more pedestrian American transportation devices, couldn't hide their enthusiasm for the new Hemi-powered Chrysler:

Fenders that mounted to the main car body were one of several Chrysler features that other automakers had left behind by 1951.

Road & Track's test crew seldom gets excited about American cars, but then *Road & Track* readers are familiar with this attitude. The Chrysler is an exception. While it has faults, and some of them are serious, we feel that it is outstanding among local efforts. . . . The tremendous performance of this V-8 is enough in itself to be a strong selling point for the Chrysler. Regardless of the rest of the car's advantages or disadvantages, when you touch that throttle, you know something mighty impressive is happening under that hood.

Road & Track wasn't the only magazine to rave about the performance of the Hemi-powered Chryslers. In a *Motor Trend* comparison test of 15 cars from the 1951 model year, the Chrysler V-8 beat the second-place Oldsmobile V-8 by a score of 176 points to 153.5 points. The magazine concluded: "It cost the Chrysler Corporation a lot of money to build the new V-8; it took a lot of courage to flout tradition and experiment with design. The award winner is, in concept, a major step ahead in American automotive history."

NASCAR

At the same time, the Hemi was already well on its way to becoming a legend on the race track: America's dirt ovals were the setting of the new and increasingly popular sport of stock car racing—that is, races in which stock-bodied production cars competed. This all-American form of racing had its base in the southeastern quadrant of the country, thanks to an enterprising mechanic named William France Sr., who had moved from Washington, D.C., to Daytona Beach, Florida, during the Great Depression. France hatched a scheme to turn stock car racing into a profitable business. In 1948, together with a group of racers and promoters, France created the National Association for Stock Car Automobile Racing (NASCAR) Grand National series. A hot production engine like Chrysler's new Hemi was tailor-made for this type of racing.

By the time of the Hemi's debut in 1951, NASCAR racing had grown so popular that it was expanding out beyond its southern roots. On August 12, 1951, the budding series came to Detroit for the first time, in the form of the inaugural Motor City 250. Held on a 1-mile dirt track at the Michigan State Fairgrounds near the intersection of Woodward Avenue and Eight Mile Road, this race marked the first time that many auto industry executives would be able to see Bill France's NASCAR extravaganza in all of its whiskey-tripping glory.

It also marked the first ever NASCAR Grand National win for a Hemi-powered Chrysler. Howard W. "Tommy" Thompson, an engineer from Louisville, Kentucky, took the checkered flag in a New Yorker coupe, beating Curtis Turner in a Rocket 88. Watching the epic battle between Turner and Thompson—complete with Turner's Olds giving Thompson's Chrysler a little love tap, sending both drivers temporarily off the track—ignited a great deal of interest in factory NASCAR participation.

Big, buff, and rugged, the 1951 Saratoga could be made into a durable, honest race car. Using the same 331-cubic-inch Hemi engine as the New Yorker, but with a six-inch shorter wheelbase, it was some 250 pounds lighter than the bigger car. Lightness means speed.

Hood latches have been known to come loose when a race car is bouncing around at speed, presenting the driver with an unwelcome set of challenges. Leather straps and sturdy metal buckles were far more resistant to accidental opening.

THE MEXICAN ROAD RACE

Almost overnight, the new Chrysler engine stirred interest from all levels of motorsports. A New Yorker convertible was selected as the pace car for the 1951 Indianapolis 500. This would be the first of several Hemi-powered cars that would pace the fabled Memorial Day Classic—in 1954 a Dodge Royal 500 paced the race and in 1956 a DeSoto Pacesetter held the honor.

Further south, La Carrera Panamericana (the Mexican Road Race, or Pan Am), was another event that allowed drivers to capitalize on the power of Chrysler's amazing new engine. The Mexican government organized the race, which was so popular that in 1954 it comprised one fourth of the world's Sports Car Championship (along with the Mille Miglia in Italy, the 24-Hours Nurburgring in Germany, and the 24 Hours of Le Mans in France). First held in 1950, La Carrera Panamericana took place in nine stages along a 2,176-mile stretch of the newly completed Pan American Highway. In 1951 Bill Sterling drove a nearly bone-stock Saratoga to a first-in-class finish, and third overall, behind a pair of Ferraris.

Despite this promising start, Chryslers didn't fare well in the next two Pan Ams. Lincoln had introduced a new OHV V-8 for 1952, and Lincolns won the stock car class in 1952 and 1953. Chrysler again took top honors in the small stock car class (the stock car division had been subdivided between passenger cars, small U.S. stock cars, and European stock cars) when Tommy Drisdale won in a Dodge. The year 1954 marked the last time the incredibly dangerous race would be run. The era of racing on public roads was coming to an end.

continued on page 61

Badges of honor, circa 1951. Owners treasured the window decals that they could display after an event as proof to their peers that they had "been there, done that."

In 1951, serious racers mounted Halibrand magnesium wheels. Lightweight, strong, and stylish, they were required for all racers, whether actual or the bench variety.

The Saratoga Club Coupe didn't wear as much brightwork as the New Yorker. Beefy bumpers could nudge another car out of the way, or, when competing in Mexico, push aside a tumbleweed.

The tiny gauges weren't the best way to monitor conditions under the hood, but a trained ear could detect trouble in seconds. The Saratoga's huge steering wheel helped with low speed maneuvering, as power steering was of the two-arm system.

Being a Chrysler, back-up lights were standard on the Saratoga Club Coupe. If you wanted to pay extra for items like that, you bought a Plymouth or Dodge.

Virgil Exner's design touches were all over the 1955 Imperial Newport, such as the constant radius wheel openings and the restrained brightwork.

The 1955 Imperial Newport's taillights looked like they were pulled straight off of the *K-310*. They brought a touch of fantasy to America's garages. More sculpture than stoplight, the feature was susceptible to the elements, but it looked straight out of Buck Rogers.

The huge valve covers with the spark plug wire channels are the most obvious visual clue that this is a 331 cubic-inch hemi. Rated at 250-horsepower, it used a Carter carburetor, hydraulic valve lifters, and an 8.5:1 compression ratio.

continued from page 54

SAME OLD SAME OLD

Unfortunately, Chrysler was unable to capitalize on the excitement generated by the new Hemi engine. Not even a world-beating engine could pull the company out of the mud bog that was the 1952 model year. Chrysler had coasted on its prewar styling for far too long. By the early 1950s all the U.S. automakers that were still viable were producing cars with styling that made Chrysler's offerings look like the warmed-over prewar boxes they were. While other manufacturers' dealerships received modern-looking cars for the 1952 model year, Chrysler dealers were stuck with cars that looked exactly like the 1951 models, their

When an interior is said to be roomy, the 1955 Imperial Newport could be used as an illustration. Power steering made spinning the large steering wheel a one-finger operation. Metal, leather, and glass; not a bit of plastic in sight.

Power everything; that was the Imperial way. From seats to windows, if it could have power assist, Chrysler installed it. Imperial owners never had to exert themselves.

only stylistic update consisting of new taillight surrounds. (To be fair, the new taillights did incorporate back-up lights.)

This lack of change was in part by design; Chrysler used the 1952 model year to synchronize its new model releases with the rest of the industry and in a way wrote off the entire model year. Ever since the war had ended, the company had been introducing new models during the calendar year in which they were labeled. Meanwhile, all the other automakers were unveiling their new cars three months earlier, in the fall of the previous year, as was the tradition for the U.S. auto market. For the 1952 model year, Chrysler deliberately didn't put much effort into restyling cars that were destined to be something very much like sacrificial goats.

As it turned out, 1952 would be the year when Chrysler would finally pay the price for its conservative-to-the-point-of-regressive approach. K.T. Keller may have gone against his character when he had personally approved the Hemi engine project, but when it came to styling and design, he kept a death grip on the corporate purse strings. In 1952, the American car-buying public made the consequences of this folly painfully clear. In 1951 Chrysler division sold 162,916 cars; in 1952 that number fell to 120,678. Clearly change was needed. Fortunately, that change had already begun to take place, in the form of Tex Colbert and Virgil Exner.

continued on page 70

Rich materials and eye-catching design were expected.

Looking not a little like a portion of the *K-310* concept car, the 1955 Imperial Newport used flowing curves and contrasting colors to move the coupe visually upmarket. Note the discrete badge at the base of the C-pillar.

Chrysler didn't introduce restyled cars with modern body work until 1955—a full ten years after the war had ended, and five years after other U.S. automakers had done so.

By the mid-1950s, designers, including Virgil
Exner, were applying more and more chrome work
to their vehicles. The rear of the Imperial Newport
shows how the taillight, back-up lamps, and
exhaust tips were all highlighted by brightwork.

Beautifully proportioned, the 1955 Imperial Newport coupe was a luxurious automobile, fit for a trip to the bank or the opera. Chrysler built only 2,094 of these fine machines.

Virgil Exner surrounded the Imperial Newport with chrome, with a bright strip tracing each wheel arch and connecting beneath the doors. The large chrome area behind the rear wheels was intended to deflect road debris, rather than risk chipping the paint.

The brake lights glowed when the driver depressed the brake pedal. Via the rear-view mirror, the driver could see a soft glow from the taillight assembly, as the center section was plastic and let some light spill forward.

Layers of chromed surfaces overlapped, resulting in a rolling piece of sculpture. Cleaning that much chrome was a challenge, but that's what you hired people to do.

In the 1950s, it was easy to ascertain a car's relative status by the amount of chrome at the front of the hood. The 1955 Imperial Newport was clearly an important vehicle.

A large speedometer kept track of the Imperial Newport's speed; this was a handy feature, since the car's smooth ride and quiet interior could lull drivers into thinking they were traveling slower than they actually were.

continued from page 62

ADVANCED STYLING

Lester Lum "Tex" Colbert began his career as a lawyer, working for a firm used by Walter P. Chrysler. He and Chrysler hit it off, and Colbert eventually became the president of Chrysler's Dodge division. K.T. Keller shared his predecessor's enthusiasm for Colbert. In fact, as Keller neared retirement, he groomed Colbert to be his replacement. Following the outbreak of the Korean War in 1950, the Pentagon selected Keller to head the U.S. missile program, and on November 3, 1950, Colbert assumed the reins of Chrysler Corporation. Keller remained on, however, as the chairman of Chrysler's board, a position that had remained vacant since Walter P. Chrysler's death in 1940.

Colbert knew that the company needed to supplant its stodgy prewar designs with modern automobiles, so his first order of business was to commission the immediate redesign of all passenger cars. Unfortunately, the realities of manufacturing automobiles dictate that "immediately" translates to three or four years down the road—and that's in the best of circumstances. Thanks to Keller's slavish devotion to stylistic entropy, Colbert's position hardly qualified as the best of circumstances.

All was not completely lost, however, because Colbert's staff already had just the man to lead Chrysler into the era of modern design. The year before he stepped down, K.T. Keller had hired a brilliant designer named Virgil Exner. With an eye toward the future, Keller set Exner up in an advanced styling studio, giving him the opportunity to work relatively free of the constraints placed on stylists by the company's engineers. Walter P. Chrysler had always appreciated good engineers, placing them in most of the top executive positions within his company. By the early 1950s, engineering's power over styling generally took the form of Henry King, who was responsible for production designs at the time Exner came on board.

In many ways, Exner was the perfect man to implement Colbert's directive to take Chrysler styling in a new direction. From 1934 until 1938, he'd headed Pontiac's design department, working for Harley Earl, who is generally considered to be the founder of automotive design. In 1938 he went to work for Raymond Loewy, whose eponymous firm designed everything from Lucky Strikes cigarette packages to Greyhound buses. At Loewy, Exner designed cars for Studebaker. In 1947 Raymond Loewy fired him for designing Studebaker's new 1947 models behind Loewy's back. Exner had actually been working at the insistence of the firm's client, who believed Loewy's interference would keep the redesign from being finished on time. Whatever the circumstances, Exner found himself in the position of freelance designer, and Keller hired him in 1949.

Loewy might not have been pleased with Exner's work on the 1947 Studebakers, but everyone else was. When the new Studebakers hit the moribund postwar U.S. auto market, their futuristic styling motivated other manufacturers to develop modern designs.

Lester Lum "Tex" Colbert. *Copyright Chrysler LLC. Used with permission.*

Exner took a Gestalt approach to designing automobiles. He believed in working with the car as a whole unit, rather than a collection of parts. In a presentation to the Society of Automotive Engineers on January 14–15, 1952, Exner summed up this approach:

> An automobile cannot be properly styled unless it is first conceived as a whole unit. . . . The theme must be a single one to which all components are intimately related. Concentration on various parts such as fenders, tops, front end, etc., is not possible until the overall picture is clearly established.

Cleanly styled, the 1951 *K-310* concept car was a radical departure for Chrysler, especially the lowered stance. The airy greenhouse and extensive use of windows filled the interior with light, and the restrained use of brightwork accented the progressive lines. *Copyright Chrysler LLC. Used with permission.*

ITALIAN SIMPLICITY

The 1952 Chryslers might have been shockingly status quo, but that didn't mean Exner was sitting on his stylish thumbs. His influence on product design was minimal in the early years, because Henry King and his engineering staff viewed Exner as a usurper and severely limited his design input. It was because of King's attempt to marginalize Exner that the advanced design studio was located off-site. In a way this was the best thing that could have happened to Exner and to Chrysler. Without the constraints of designing cars for production, Exner was free to create the ultimate expressions of his design aesthetic. Together with Maury Baldwin and Cliff Voss, Exner's little advanced design studio created cars that represented genuine breakthroughs in automotive design. Exner and company used this creative freedom to build a series of one-off cars that would travel to Chrysler dealerships around the country, showing dealers and customers alike that the company would eventually produce something other than the prewar transportation boxes currently taking up space on showroom floors.

The first of those advanced design exercises to become a chrome-and-steel reality was the *K-310*. Exner's team designed the *K-310* in Detroit but it was built by Carrozzeria Ghia in Turin, Italy. This was in part to ensure secrecy and keep the project off of King's radar, but the farming out of the *K-310* project was also the result of Chrysler's devoting all available resources to military production because of the ongoing war in Korea.

This stylish four-seat sports coupe proved a rolling prototype for the design sensibility that Exner would bring to Chrysler's sporty production cars in a few short years. In the above-mentioned presentation to the Society of Automotive Engineers, Exner described the influences that had shaped his vision of the *K-310*, which he defined as British-traditional, German-functional, French-flamboyant, and Italian-simplicity. "Sometimes we become too

The prominent outline of the spare tire on the *K-310* trunk lid was a stylistic element that would show up on a number of Virgil Exner designs. Two-tone paint schemes were starting to attract the attention of Detroit, and as the decade progressed, many production cars would be so painted. *Copyright Chrysler LLC. Used with permission.*

Chrysler highlighted its new-for-1951 331-cubic-inch Hemi V-8 by installing it in the futuristic *K-310* concept car. Virgil Exner designed the car in America but commissioned Ghia in Italy to build it. *Copyright Chrysler LLC. Used with permission.*

The small chromed grill was a Ghia design signature, and it ran counter to the huge openings found on Detroit's production vehicles. The absence of brightwork set the *K-310* apart from most concept cars, which tended to have excessive chrome. *Copyright Chrysler LLC. Used with permission.*

Frameless window glass was one of the advanced design elements used on the 1951 *K-310*. The large door opening allowed for relatively easy access to the rear seating area. Note the split front bench seat, which allowed each front occupant to position their seat for their comfort. *Copyright Chrysler LLC. Used with permission.*

preoccupied with our Detroit designs," Exner told the assembled crowd, "and fail to take note of what the other fellow is doing."

One of the most influential features of the *K-310* was its long hood and short rear deck, elements that would come to define the cars of the classic muscle-car era a generation later. Exner extolled the functional virtues of such a design. He believed the long hood allowed better access to the engine compartment and that a short deck moved the passenger compartment back, placing more weight on the rear wheels for better traction and balance. He also understood the effect a long hood and short deck had on people viewing the design. In his January 1952 speech to the Society of Automotive Engineers, he explained: "The long hood is a potent psychological factor in that it denotes power and strong directional quality."

That, and it just plain looks cool. Ford would adopt this design for its Mustang production car a dozen years after Exner's speech, and in so doing, would dictate the expectations of performance car buyers from that point forward.

By using a spring on the spare tire mounting bracket, the weight of the wheel/tire combination was easily overcome, allowing anyone to remove the tire with ease. When stowed, the tire would fill the well in the floor of the trunk. *Copyright Chrysler LLC. Used with permission.*

The 1951 *K-310's* graceful lines were years ahead of their time. Top-range Chrysler products later in the decade would use this same taillight assembly. *Copyright Chrysler LLC. Used with permission.*

This is mid-twentieth century living at its best! It's 1955, and with a Chrysler New Yorker Deluxe Town & Country station wagon in the driveway, the neighbors will know you have arrived.

THE HOT ROD BOYS

James Zeder, who became Chrysler's vice president of engineering in 1951 when his brother Fred died, initially showed little more interest in developing the Hemi's vast reserves of untapped performance potential than K.T. Keller and Henry King showed in developing updated body styles. But engineers are engineers, and ultimately Zeder became infected with the enthusiasm generated by the group of engineers whom he called "the hot rod boys." Zeder gave engineering the go-ahead to experiment with high-performance versions of the Hemi.

With a 331.1-cubic-inch Hemi under the hood, this big wagon didn't take long to get to the weekend camping spot. Rated at 250 horsepower, it delivered plenty of steam for heading up into the mountains.

Kids, bring out the rest of the luggage! The huge tailgate supports plenty of weight for those football game get-togethers, and the abundance of chrome helped to celebrate the good life.

Plenty of room for the entire family. Chrome stripes on the floor and rear seat back protected the surface from abrasions. Why, you could put a whole week's worth of groceries back there!

A full bench seat was a bit utilitarian, but power assist let the driver position the large seat effortlessly.

Just because you're driving a station wagon doesn't mean you have to forgo style. The owner of this 1955 Chrysler New Yorker Deluxe Town & Country enjoys a styled interior, complete with a two-tone steering wheel and dashboard.

An impressive hood ornament announced the car's presence while also making an ideal handhold when lifting the heavy hood. The big wagon tipped the scales at 4,430 pounds.

They began by raising compression ratios. With no other changes but a bump in the compression ratio to 12.5:1, they coaxed 228 horsepower from a stock 331 engine, but that required the use of fuel with an octane rating of 130 or better. This route was out of the question, because Zeder dictated that all production versions of the engine would run on regular pump gas. As he'd told the Society of Automotive Engineers in 1951:

> We at Chrysler Corporation are in favor of increasing compression ratios as fast as higher-octane fuels become commercially available. In the interests of economy and savings to the consumer, we intend in the future to use the highest compression which will permit smooth operation with regularly available fuels. But at the same time we intend to pursue all other avenues of increasing engine performance and economy. . . . The hemispherical combustion chamber not only makes [the Hemi engine] the most efficient engine available today (in terms of pounds of fuel used per brake horsepower hour), but it also makes it better able to take advantage of better fuels [that] will be developed in the future.

Chrysler built just 1,036 New Yorker Deluxe Town & Country station wagons for the 1955 model year. The car's hefty price tag of $4,208 probably kept a few people from making the investment.

From the front, the Town & Country station wagon was instantly identifiable as a 1955 Chrysler. Layered chrome strips above the front bumper gave the vehicle a low and wide stance.

A long rear overhang required the driver to use special care to avoid scraping the dual exhaust tips on steep driveways.

The development team began working on a version of the engine that had better flow into and out of the combustion chambers. This engine, dubbed the K-310, the same moniker given to Exner's styling exercise of the same period, featured a set of tuned tubular headers in place of the stock Hemi's exhaust manifolds, leading to an increase of 13 horsepower (to 193) and 18 lb-ft of torque (to 330 lb-ft).

Next they polished the intake and exhaust ports and installed bigger valves, with 2.06-inch valves in the intake ports and 1.625-inch valves in the exhaust ports. They developed a manifold that allowed the use of four one-barrel downdraft carburetors, and they used an electronic computer to determine the ultimate cam profiles. With 7.0:1 compression pistons the K-310 engine generated 308 horsepower and 361 lb-ft of torque. When 12.5:1 compression pistons were installed, the engine cranked out 353 horsepower and 385 lb-ft of torque. Using the lessons learned from the K-310 test engine, Chrysler bumped the power of the production FirePower engine to 190 for the 1952 model year.

That same year DeSoto introduced a 276-cubic-inch version of the Hemi engine. Like its bigger Chrysler brother, the DeSoto Hemi featured an oversquare bore and stroke ratio, in this case the bore being 3.625 inches and the stroke being 3.440 inches. Intake valves measured 1.84 inches across, and 1.5-inch units served duty in the exhaust ports. With a 7.0:1 compression ratio and a two-barrel carburetor, the DeSoto Hemi pumped out 160 horsepower and 250 lb-ft of torque. With the advent of the Hemi engine, DeSoto dropped the Deluxe and Custom nameplates from its cars

With its retractable rear window, the Town & Country was able to swallow long loads. It was a graceful solution to what could have been an ugly, utilitarian device.

Chrome accents were the automobile designer's best friend, as evidenced on the 1955 Chrysler New Yorker Deluxe Town & Country station wagon. The taillight assembly was an exquisitely shaped piece, and even the bumper contour was echoed in a thin line of chrome.

and renamed the six-cylinder version the Powermaster and the V-8 version the FireDome, in honor of its Hemi engine.

In 1953 Dodge introduced its version of the Hemi, the Red Ram. This engine, the smallest version of the original Hemi, at 241 cubic inches, differed quite a bit from its larger brethren. Like the FireDome, it featured a compression ratio of 7.0:1, and like both the DeSoto and Chrysler engines, it used a two-barrel carburetor. But with a bore and stroke of just 3.4375 inches and 3.250 inches, respectively, the combustion chambers were much more compact, requiring the use of smaller valves. The Red Ram used 1.75-inch intake valves and 1.41-inch exhaust valves.

That same year Bob Rodger began development of a clandestine project—a stylish, sporty car that would mate Virgil Exner's styling to a powerful Hemi engine. The Exner body and Hemi engine would be mounted on a chassis with a sophisticated suspension, giving the car handling prowess to match its looks and acceleration. This car would become the C-300.

THE COMPETITION HEATS UP

These Hemis of 1953 were great engines, but by that time the FirePower no longer occupied the top slot in the American V-8 performance hierarchy. That honor belonged to Cadillac, which had increased the output of its OHV V-8 to 210 horsepower. That year Cadillac beat Chrysler in the NASCAR race at Daytona.

Chrysler changed little of the Imperial's front for 1956, but Exner's team did make the rear fenders taller. More significantly, the engine department enlarged the Hemi engine to 353.1 cubic inches, which translated into a power increase from 250 to 280 horsepower.

"Gunsight" taillights were carried over from the 1955 model. Meanwhile, the "fin wars" were starting to heat up.

Worse for Chrysler, other General Motors divisions were producing V-8 engines that nearly equaled the output of Chrysler's once-dominant Hemi. The Oldsmobile Rocket engine now cranked out 165 horsepower, and Buick had introduced a new OHV V-8 that generated 188 horsepower.

For 1954 Chrysler increased the output of the two-barrel FirePower to 195 horsepower and offered a four-barrel version that produced 235 horsepower. This barely put the Chrysler engine ahead of the Cadillac, which was bumped up to 230 horsepower for the 1954 model year. But all the other manufacturers also increased the outputs of their OHV V-8 engines. The Buick increased to 200 horsepower, the Olds increased to 185 horsepower, the DeSoto increased to 170 horsepower, and the Dodge increased to 150 horsepower. With an aftermarket manifold manufactured by Offenhauser and sold through Dodge parts departments, output of the Dodge Red Ram could be increased to an estimated 180 horsepower. Even stodgy old Ford was getting in on the act, finally replacing its antiquated side-valve V-8 with a slightly less antiquated OHV engine. This 239-cubic-inch unit generated 130 horsepower. It wasn't much, but it helped power Ford well ahead of Chrysler in the marketplace.

The Chrysler Hemis were still more than competitive on the track. Lee Petty won the Daytona race in 1954, putting the superior power of the Hemi engine in his New Yorker to good use, taking pole position with a qualifying speed of 123.4 miles per hour. (Petty didn't cross the

Like any automobile manufacturer, Chrysler recommended that owners use genuine factory parts and service, including approved windshield washer fluid. One of the advantages to having the washer fluid in a bag was that it was a snap to see how full the reservoir was.

Elegant in black, the 1956 Imperial rode on a long 133-inch wheelbase, and weighed in at 4,555 pounds. Priced at a lofty $5,094, Chrysler made just 2,094 two-door hardtops.

The black metal strip running across the FirePower V-8's valve cover concealed the spark plug wires. This unusual design was required due to the spark plug's central location in the combustion chamber; the spark plug wire lead extended down through the cylinder head.

finish line first—Oldsmobile driver Tim Flock took the checkered flag, but Flock's Olds was disqualified when a postrace tech inspection uncovered an illegally modified carburetor.) Petty took first in seven races that season and went on to give Chrysler its first ever NASCAR Grand National championship.

As powerful as the Hemis were, everyone involved with developing the engine knew the engines could be much more powerful. Given the tremendous untapped potential of the Hemi design, it seemed ridiculous to engage in incremental leapfrogging with the other manufacturers, when it would be a simple matter to make a Hemi so powerful that it would take the other manufacturers years to catch up. And Chrysler's engineers knew just how to build such an engine, thanks in large part to development work done to help out a racer and sports car builder named Briggs Cunningham.

THE A311

In 1907 Briggs Swift Cunningham II was born into a wealthy Cincinnati banking family. His uncle indoctrinated him at an early age him into the cult of motorsports by taking him street racing in a Dodge powered by an Hispano-Suiza aircraft engine. Cunningham became a racing junky and enjoyed a mildly successful career racing sports cars, but he dreamed of something more—his goal was to field a team of American cars with American drivers who would win the fabled 24 Hours of Le Mans race in France.

Cunningham tried to achieve this goal in 1950 by fielding his Fordillac, a Frankenstein creation that mated a Cadillac V-8 with a lightweight Ford chassis. The organizations sanctioning the Le Mans race rejected his car because they didn't consider it a production vehicle, so Cunningham bought two Cadillac Coupe DeVilles to enter in the race. One kept the stock bodywork, but the other featured a body that had been cobbled together by employees of the Grumman Aircraft factory.

Cunningham's cars finished tenth and eleventh that year, a result decent enough to earn the respect of French fans, but Cunningham wanted more. He recognized the potential of the Hemi engine and decided to use that powerplant in his new C-2, a car that Cunningham was building to race at Le Mans in 1951. Cunningham spent a then-staggering $100,000 to build the car, which featured coil-spring suspension at all four corners and a de Dion independent rear suspension. Unfortunately, the car (and the Hemi engine) were heavy, weighing about 700 pounds more than the C-2's closest competitors, and Cunningham finished 18th overall.

When Briggs Cunningham built the C-4R, his second Hemi-powered racecar for the 24 Hours of Le Mans, he abandoned the heavy de Dion independent rear suspension used on the C-2R in favor of a lighter Chrysler live axle. He felt the extra weight of the de Dion wasn't worth any performance advantages it might offer.

The C-4R retained the Ford-sourced A-arm-and-coil-spring setup used on the C-2R. While the C-2R had been a rushed project, Cunningham had plenty of time to develop the C-4R. Cunningham himself drove one of the cars for 20 of the 24 hours at the 1952 Le Mans race. He hogged most of the seat time because he was nursing a weak clutch and didn't want his more aggressive co-driver Bill Spear to fry the clutch completely.

To provide Cunningham with a competitive engine, a team of Chrysler engineers that included John Platner and Don Moore began working on the A311 engine program. The A311 program, which would become the foundation for most of Chrysler's racing engines throughout the 1950s, represented the state of the engine-building art at that time. In its ultimate form, it featured gear-driven camshafts with roller tappets that had extreme lift and duration numbers, a 12:1 compression ratio (no dictates about using pump gas here), aluminum racing pistons, Hillborn fuel injection with tuned velocity stacks, special pushrods, and dual valve springs with surge dampeners. Testing revealed that the engine was so strong that it was flexing the block, so the engineering team mounted a bracing plate between the block and the oil pan for added structural rigidity.

Cunningham further developed his cars for 1952, now labeled the C-4Rs, shedding some 600 pounds from the overall weight of the car and engine package. The FirePower engine now generated 300 reliable horsepower. Unfortunately, the five-speed transmissions Cunningham installed in the cars didn't prove as reliable as the engines; they suffered lubrication problems under racing conditions, and Cunningham was forced to substitute Cadillac three-speed transmissions at the last minute. This put the C-4Rs at a tremendous disadvantage when braking down Le Mans' long straights, but even though two of the three cars Cunningham entered broke down and didn't finish the race, the third car, driven by Cunningham himself, finished a respectable fourth.

In 1953 Cunningham had to reduce the compression ratio of the A311 to 7.5:1 in order to use the mandated French gasoline, but he still drove his C-5R to a podium finish, taking third overall. In 1954 Cunningham entered two C-4Rs, each powered by 330-horsepower A311 engines, and his drivers finished third and fifth overall. Cunningham might not have achieved his dream of winning at Le Mans, but he did manage to outrun all but a handful of factory-sponsored teams while trying.

INDIANAPOLIS 500

Chrysler engineers were pleased with Cunningham's results in France, but they had their eyes set on a prize a little closer to home: the Indianapolis 500. They developed a version of the A311 that generated over 400 horsepower. When mounted in a Kurtis Kraft racing chassis, this engine/car combination averaged over 135 miles per hour in testing at the Indianapolis Motor Speedway. The engine was rugged enough for the Memorial Day race too, running for 900 miles at a stretch without needing so much as a change of spark plugs.

These results were perhaps too impressive; they scared the powers that be, and at the last minute the sanctioning bodies lowered the displacement limit for the Indianapolis 500 to 275 cubic inches. Chrysler experimented with a 271-cubic-inch version of the A311, but they didn't have enough time to make it competitive.

Chrysler engineers got their revenge, though. When Chrysler opened its Chelsea Proving Grounds in 1954, the company invited the top four finishers from that year's Indy 500 to test the cars they had used at Indy on the high-banked 4.7-mile track, which allowed drivers to maintain wide-open throttle over the entire course. The fastest lap turned in by the four drivers was 179 miles per hour. Then Chrysler brought out a Kurtis Kraft roadster powered by an A311 racing engine and proceeded to lap the track at 182 miles per hour.

The A311 played another notable role—influencing Tom Hoover, who would go on to become the godfather of the 426 Hemi. In an interview published in the August 2005 issue of *Hot Rod*, Hoover told the magazine:

> The thing that was the most significant to me was the A311 program that explored the potential of the Chrysler 331 Hemi as a potential Indianapolis 500 racing engine. The A311 report became the most desirable reading material among those of us enrolled in the Chrysler Institute. I graduated from the Chrysler Institute in 1957 and at about the same time a group of Chrysler employees formed the Ram Chargers group, a loose knit bunch of engineers who drag raced their cars on weekends. Even though the A311 program didn't produce an Indy victory due to USAC rule changes, the technical report it generated was a guiding light for me. ■

CHAPTER TWO

"WE CAN'T AFFORD ANOTHER MISTAKE"

"WE CAN'T AFFORD ANOTHER MISTAKE"

When the 1955 Chryslers hit the market, one model in the lineup—the C-300—would be so groundbreaking that its influence on both performance and styling would be felt for generations to come.

Chrysler was the last company anyone would have pegged to produce such an innovative design. While other manufacturers had been changing to suit the times—building cars that were longer, lower, and wider—Chrysler maintained the stately, upright proportions of its prewar cars. It took something akin to an automotive apocalypse to get Chrysler to abandon the boxy styling that K.T. Keller had locked onto like a pit bull on a hambone. That apocalypse came in the form of 1954 sales figures. Total Chrysler sales plummeted from 170,006 cars in 1953 to 104,985 cars in 1954. Dodge and Plymouth numbers were even worse than Chrysler's. The public wanted longer, lower, wider cars, and if Chrysler

Page 96-97: When designing the 1957 300C, Virgil Exner took a very different approach than he had when designing the earlier versions of the car. The car's aggressive stance shows how Italian design was influencing Exner at the time.

Page 98-99: (Main) The theme of excess continued under the hood of the 300C; Chrysler enlarged the Hemi engine to 392 cubic inches and bumped output to 375 horsepower in the twin four-barrel version. *(Inset)* Exner was one of the greatest proponents of tailfins in the U.S. auto industry, and many people feel his tailfin designs were the best executed.

In 1955 America, the C-300 was the most powerful new production vehicle available. A two-ton, six-passenger coupe, it was a low-production model; only 1,725 units were built.

wouldn't provide them, well they could just drive their old-fart cars straight to hell as fast as their overachieving Hemi engines could carry them.

When the numbers came in, Keller finally understood that he had been wrong to try to block design progress at Chrysler. He told the *Detroit Free Press:* "I have seen the error of my ways. Christ, we can't afford another mistake." Chrysler was finally ready to implement some of Virgil Exner's revolutionary styling ideas. In his book *Chrysler & Imperial 1946-1975: The Classic Postwar Years* (Motorbooks, 1975), author Richard M. Langworth recounts a meeting between Keller and Exner, as described by Exner's son, Virgil Jr.:

> There came the day when K.T. Keller asked Dad's opinion on what the 1955 stuff was going to look like. Dad told him "lousy." K.T. kind of liked that— [Keller] was quite a strong character.
>
> "Okay," he said, "you put it together and you've got 18 months." They quickly swiped ideas off the parade cars [Exner's design exercises, or "idea cars," as he called them] and managed to put the 1955 line together in time.

Metal and lots of it. Vehicles in the mid-1950s were truly rolling sculptures. Though the emphasis on the C-300 was performance, it was a treat for the eyes as well.

With dual Carter four-barrel carburetors, solid lifters, and a full-race camshaft, the C-300's 331.1-cubic-inch Hemi was rated at 300 horsepower at 5,200 rpm. It made a delicious roar under full throttle.

Exner based the styling of the 1955 lineup on the *Parade Phaeton*, a show car he had created in 1952 using a Crown Imperial chassis. The new models from Chrysler had the long, low, clean lines that customers of the day demanded. The crown jewel in the new line was the C-300, which made its debut on February 8, 1955.

"THE MOST POWERFUL SEDAN IN THE WORLD"

Bob Rodger headed the C-300 development team. A serious race fan, Rodger had been inspired to build a more sporting Chrysler by watching the Mexican Race and Briggs Cunningham's cars in the early 1950s. In the first weeks of August 1954, Rodger approached Ed Quinn, the general manager of Chrysler division, about the sporty car project he had been developing on the sly for more than a year.

The C-300's nose emblem displays Chrysler's on-track ambitions for its high-powered luxury car. Large twin egg crate grills let plenty of cooling air flow through the radiator.

Chrysler offered the 1955 C-300 in just three colors: black, Platinum white, and Tango red. Stylist Virgil Exner preferred a clean, "European" look, and the C-300 benefited from his restraint.

Due to its heavy-duty suspension, the 1955 C-300 sat one inch lower than other Chryslers using the same basic platform. While improved handling was a welcome result, the aggressive stance wasn't to be underestimated.

The 1955 C-300 exhibited a purity of line not seen in many American vehicles of that era. Unfortunately, in the following years, vehicle designs would emulate rocket ships, resulting in some creations that would prove to be memorable—for all the wrong reasons.

Soft leather covered the huge front and rear bench seats. The seat backs in the front tilted forward to allow access to the rear.

Grasping the C-300's huge two-tone steering wheel was like holding the controls of a powerful 1950s speedboat.

Quinn told Rodger that he could develop his sporty car project, but specified that he couldn't deviate in any expensive fashion from the 1955 production models, which were about to hit the showroom in a couple of months. The 1954 disaster had cleared out Chrysler's coffers, forcing the company to borrow operating money from Prudential to survive. Needless to say, there wasn't a lot of fat in the budget for expensive die changes for pet projects. Because of this, the C-300 was a prime example of parts-bin engineering. Exner, Cliff Voss, and Tom Poirier selected a New Yorker hardtop body and Windsor rear quarter panels. The grille, parking lights, and front bumper came from the Imperial. As production neared, Exner made some last minute tweaks. He replaced the Imperial bumpers—which he considered too bulky for a sporting car—with more slender Chrysler bumpers and parking lights.

Chrysler entered C-300s in the 1955 Daytona Speed Week competitions. Unsurprisingly, the 300-horsepower machines took all three leading positions in the American Stock Car Flying Mile competition, clocking a top speed of 127.58 miles per hour.

The C-300 may have been an example of parts-bin engineering, but the resulting car was stunningly beautiful. Apparently parts-bin engineering works when the parts are as good as those that Exner's team had at their disposal.

While Exner handled styling chores, Rodger concentrated on engine development. His foundation was a stock 331-cubic-inch Hemi block, which had been redesigned for the 1955 model year, with altered water passages to improve cooling. To the block he added the steep cam from the A311 race engine program, and installed solid lifters, 8.5:1 compression pistons,

Riding on a 126-inch wheelbase, the 1955 C-300 had an overall length of 218.8 inches, more than enough to fill most garages. Six-volt electrical systems were the norm for the era; hence the head and taillights were slightly less than brilliant.

The "C" in C-300 stood for Coupe, and the Exner-design displayed superb proportions. Although no one realized it at the time, this was the start of the muscle car era.

and bigger valves, and then mounted a second four-barrel carburetor. The result was the 300-horsepower engine that gave the C-300 its name.

This engine didn't just represent an incremental improvement over the competition; it was a giant leap ahead. No matter how one measured performance, the C-300 was the fastest car on the road in 1955. Only the Cadillac Eldorado came close. Its V-8 generated 270 horsepower, but the Eldorado weighed 1,000 pounds more than the C-300. This left the C-300 in a class of one. (Packard had introduced an OHV V-8 for 1955 that pumped out 275 horsepower, but Packard was in such dire financial straights that its quality control processes were in the toilet, and the few cars it did sell for the 1955 model year all had

Nearly all of the front sheet metal was carried over from the 1955 C-300 to the 300B. But Chrysler did insert a "B" into the emblem gracing the new model's nose for 1956.

Two engines were offered in the 1956 300B. The standard 354-cubic-inch, 9.0:1 compression powerplant delivered 340-horsepower, while the optional mill raised the compression ratio to 10.0:1 to generate 355 ponies at 5,200 rpm.

The 1956 Chrysler 300B claimed both highest horsepower and fastest titles when it attacked the World Passenger Car Speed Record at Daytona Beach, Florida. The Hemi-powered machine averaged a speed of 133.9 miles per hour.

The only significant exterior change on the 300B was the adoption of mild tail fins, keeping in line with the trend of the times.

Well-built and comfortably appointed, the 300B was an easy car to maneuver, thanks to power steering and good visibility. Overlaying every drive was an impressive rumble from the Hemi.

At the aft end of the tail fins was a cleanly styled taillight, with a backup lamp below.

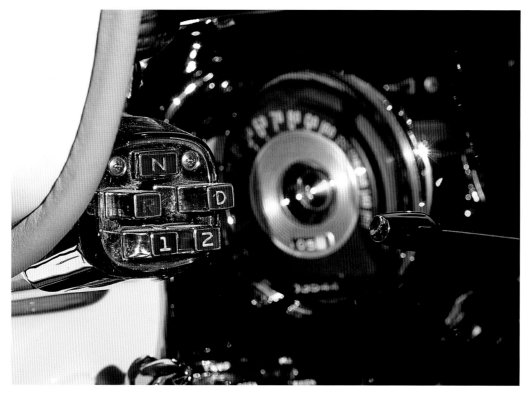

In 1956 Chrysler introduced a dash-mounted push-button shifter for the 300B's standard-equipment automatic transmission.

continued from page 114

As the fin wars escalated in the mid-1950s, the 300B's fins remained subdued and tasteful.

The 300B was certainly the fastest car built in America. The base engine, a dual-quad 354-cubic-inch Hemi with 9.0:1 compression, pumped out 340 horsepower. When equipped with optional 10.0:1 compression pistons, output jumped to 355 horsepower. This was enough to propel the car to 140 miles per hour, making it fast even by today's standards.

The C-300 had been offered with a PowerFlite automatic transmission as standard equipment. In the 300B this transmission was operated by a system of dash-mounted buttons, rather than the column-mounted stalk used the previous year. This innovation would remain a Chrysler staple into the next decade.

In response to the demands of customers who raced their 300s, Chrysler offered an optional column-shifted three-speed manual transmission. The C-300 had built a reputation as a performance icon both on the street and on the track, and Chrysler wanted to maintain that momentum. As a result, a buyer could order final drive ratios all the way up to John Deere-tractor-like 6.17:1.

The Flight Sweep rear fenders worked well with the Imperial front sheet metal to create a muscular personal car. Priced at $4,242, only 1,102 examples were made.

The sporty Adventurer was quite a departure for Chrysler's DeSoto division, which had long been considered a stodgy brand best suited for frugal octogenarians. This is a 1956 model. *Larry Zappone*

"THE GUY TO BEAT"

In 1956 Chrysler set its sights on the one remaining form of American racing that was still dominated by flathead V-8s: drag racing. Drag racers had stuck with the inefficient side-valve design for the practical reasons of cost and aftermarket support.

As spectacular a car as the 300 was, it was still too expensive and too heavy for serious hot rodders. Overhead valve V-8s might have completely taken over from their side-valve brethren when it came to the U.S. passenger car market, but there wasn't yet any speed

Clean, understated elegance and grace—this is the 1956 DeSoto Fireflite Adventurer, DeSoto's less-expensive version of the 300B muscle car. *Larry Zappone*

equipment available for them. According to Don Garlits, who was by then a budding drag racer in Florida, OHV V-8s had rev-limiting hydraulic lifters, and parts to remedy this weren't readily available on a nationwide basis. The C-300 had solid lifters, but with a price tag north of $4,000, it was beyond the financial reach of the average drag racer. In his book *Tales from the Drag Strip* (Sports Publishing LLC, 2004, co-written by Bill Stephens), Garlits writes: "I once made the stupid statement, 'Those overhead valve engines will never outrun these flatheads.'"

De Soto
most
powerful car
in the
medium-price
field !

DE SOTO DIVISION, CHRYSLER CORPORATION

255 hp Why wait for 255 hp performance in next year's cars . . . you can get it *today* in the powerful new 1956 De Soto. Here's the car that's more spirited and agile in city driving . . . safer and more comfortable at super-highway speeds . . . and costs hundreds of dollars less than you think! You'll find some De Soto models actually cost far less than dolled-up versions of the low-price three!

Your De Soto dealer is out to top his sales records of last year, and he's ready to make the deals to do it. That's why he's able to give you a truly fabulous trade-in on a big, luxurious new De Soto. Before you put a dollar down on any car . . . see and drive *and price* the smart **'56 De Soto—the car for the super-highway age.**

ace car for the 1956 Indianapolis speed classic, the new 255 hp e Soto Fireflite, will set a scorching pace for thirty-three of nerica's fastest racing cars on Memorial Day, May thirtieth!

DE SOTO OFFICIAL PACE CAR 1956 PIKES PEAK AUTO HILL CLIMB

Push-button control is the easiest way ever invented to drive or park a car. Positive mechanical control. Try it today!

High torque take-off. De Soto with its mighty 255 hp engine will give you the fastest take-off you ever experienced! It outpowers, outguns, outhandles every other car in the medium-price field!

De Soto dealers present **Groucho Marx** in "You Bet Your Life" on NBC radio and TV

DeSoto's advertising for its new 1956 Adventurer focused on the car's Fireflite Hemi engine. *David Newhardt Collection*

Introduced on February 18, 1956, the two-door Adventurer was a sub-series of the Fireflite line. The retail price for DeSoto's top-shelf offering was $3,678. *Larry Zappone*

Golden wheel covers used a turbine design in an effort to ride the jet-styling wave. Contrasting gold with white paint scheme gave the 1956 Adventurer an upscale look. *Larry Zappone*

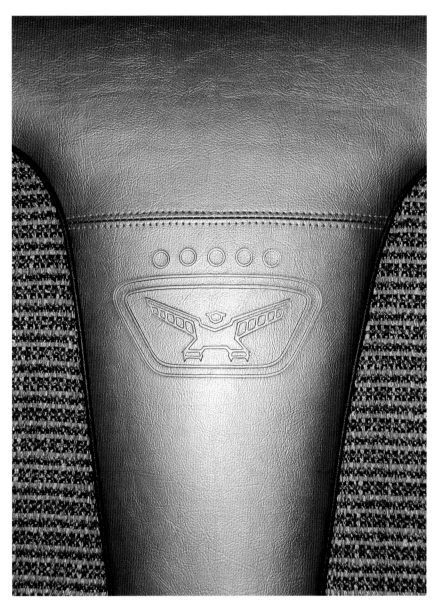

DeSoto hid the gas filler behind a door on the passenger side rear fin, capped with a "V8" emblem. By 1956, it was clear that full-sized American cars were going to be flaunting ever larger rear tail fins, à la fighter aircraft. *Larry Zappone*

DeSoto used quality interior materials in the 1956 Fireflite, and even went so far as to emboss a winged creature in the vinyl in the rear seat back cushion. *Larry Zappone*

Still, Garlits found the powerful Hemi engines useful. In the mid-1950s he bought a 331-cubic-inch Hemi from a junkyard and mounted it in the Ford coupe he used to tow his dragster to the strip. Garlits needed a strong engine because, as he wrote: "If you were towing your dragster and got behind some farmer on his tractor while you were on your way to or from the track, you needed some real power to pull out and get around him."

One day Garlits broke the transmission in his dragster. Rather than going home without racing, he decided to see what the Hemi-powered Ford coupe could do on the drag strip. When he told his wife Pat what he had in mind, she responded, "You'd better not break it, because if you do, we won't have any way to get home."

In their 1956 advertisements, DeSoto urged potential buyers to "Drive a DeSoto Before You Decide." The organizers of the 1956 Indianapolis 500 must have followed this advice, because they selected the Fireflite Adventurer to be the Official Pace Car for that year's event. *Larry Zappone*

The Fireflite Eight came equipped with dual Carter four-barrel carburetors which helped to generate 345-horsepower at 5,200 rpm. Dual oil bath air cleaners helped to keep particulate matter out of the combustion chambers. *Larry Zappone*

DeSoto understood that options could be a rich source of revenue, as well as a means for buyers to individualize their new cars. This Adventurer has been fitted with the record player option, as well as a gasoline-fired heater, and a self-winding clock in the steering wheel hub. *Larry Zappone*

Why settle for listening to the AM radio when you can relax to your favorite long-playing record album? At first glance, a record player in an automobile is crazy, but the device did work. The arm that held the needle exerted considerable pressure on the records. Needless to say, record life was limited. *Larry Zappone*

Garlits writes:

Well, I decided to give it a try anyway. I eased it to the line, and with those old 8.20x15 treaded tires on it, I had to take it easy when I left and not break them loose. I got it right, and I went through the gears and shot down the track. Now, our flathead dragster had made a full pass with a time of about 12.5 seconds at 108 mph. That coupe ran a 14-flat at 114 mph! On the way home . . . I said to Pat, "Honey, the first guy to put one of those Chrysler Hemi engines in a dragster is going to be the guy to beat."

And she said, "Well, you'd better put one in your dragster right away!" [I] didn't need to be told twice. Almost as soon as we got back, I dropped that Hemi into the dragster and couldn't wait to go up to Brooksville to see what we had. The engine still had the original ignition and a battery, it had dual-quads, and it went out and ran 10.5 seconds at 128 mph! I tell you what, the drag racing world around here was set on its ear! That kind of performance had never been seen before. I mean, with the 12.5s we had been running, we were winning Top Eliminator!

Garlits found a frame from a 1931 Chevrolet—he chose that year "because the bodies had so much wood in them that they'd rot away and you'd have the frame left over"—and built the *Swamp Rat,* his first purpose-built Hemi-powered dragster. By 1957 he had his Hemi-powered cars running through the quarter-mile at 170 miles per hour, at a time when the world record was 168.22 miles per hour.

The DeSoto Adventurer was the first vehicle in America to come equipped with a base engine that generated one horsepower per cubic inch of displacement. That works out to 345/345. *Larry Zappone*

When reports of Garlits' exploits reached drag racing's spiritual home in Southern California, the racers there scarcely believed them. They thought that the Florida tracks where Garlits raced must be using faulty clocks, but Hemi performance was about to get even more unbelievable. Garlits might not have earned a doctorate from the prestigious

When you're driving a 1956 DeSoto Adventurer, there's always plenty of room for stepping out on the town with another couple! Metallic fabrics were popular on luxury vehicles of the era. *Larry Zappone*

When the 1956 DeSoto Fireflite Pace Car was whizzing around the Indianapolis 500 track leading the field, the two-tone paint and gold-tone trim helped the car stand out from the crowd. *Larry Zappone*

A multiple-layered convertible top created a warm and cozy environment when Mother Nature dished out non-convertible weather. The raised top maintained the roof contour of the Adventurer. *Larry Zappone*

Chrysler Institute, but he possessed a natural engineering brilliance, and he instinctively understood how to tap the wealth of power hidden within Chrysler's amazing Hemi. With a little tweaking to the fuel delivery system, Garlits pushed his Hemi-powered dragster through the quarter-mile at 176.4 miles per hour in 8.79 seconds. "The Californians could believe it if they wanted to," Garlits writes.

In 1958 Garlits met three of the fastest drag racers in California at a track in Houston, Texas, and proceeded to beat each one, making believers out of the California hot rodders. Soon the gospel of the Hemi would spread from coast to coast.

MORE MOPAR MUSCLE

Resourceful hot rodders weren't the only groups taking advantage of the phenomenal performance of Chrysler's Hemi. The corporation's DeSoto and Dodge divisions soon built their own Hemi-powered muscle cars.

DeSoto's answer to the 300 series was the Adventurer. Like the 300, the Adventurer was a luxury vehicle, occupying the top rung of the DeSoto line; it even offered the unique Highway Hi-Fi turntable as an option. And like the 300, the Adventurer featured DeSoto division's most highly tuned version of the Hemi engine; DeSoto engineers extracted 320 horsepower from the 341-cubic-inch dual quad V-8. An Adventurer paced the 1956 running of the Indianapolis 500.

The lack of a B-pillar created a large side "daylight opening," giving the 1956 Adventurer a graceful profile. Climbing into and out of the rear seats could be a struggle, though, especially for a lady in an evening gown. *Larry Zappone*

Dodge division had introduced a sporting car in 1954, the Royal 500, beating the C-300 to the market by a year, but this was just a low-volume version of the division's Royal convertible with a special trim package commemorating the car's service as the pace car in the 1954 running of the Indianapolis 500. And it still featured the decidedly unsporting pre-Exner bodywork.

Instead of offering a purpose-built performance model like the 300 and Adventurer for 1956, Dodge offered a performance package that could be added as an option to any of the division's

DeSoto touted the tail fins as a stabilizing influence at high speed. The huge trunk had a low lift-over. *Larry Zappone*

models. Called the D-500, this option package boasted a tuned version of the division's Red Ram Hemi (which now displaced 315 cubic inches and produced 260 horsepower), mounted in a specially braced frame with heavy-duty suspension components. This option package quickly became a favorite with law-enforcement agencies across the country.

If a buyer wanted the ultimate performance Dodge, he or she ordered a Coronet with a manual transmission, then specified the D-500-1 option. This package substituted the stock Red Ram cam with a racing unit and mounted a pair of four-barrel carburetors to increase power to 295 horsepower.

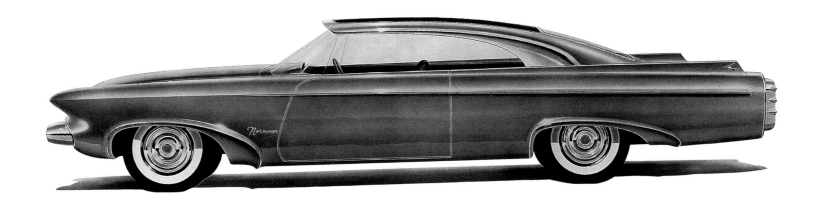

In 1956, the Chrysler-designed *Norseman* concept car was heading to America after being built by Ghia in Turin, Italy, when the Italian liner that was carrying it, the *Andrea Doria*, collided with the Swedish-American liner *Stockholm*, and sank, taking the $200,000 vehicle to the bottom of the Atlantic Ocean. *Copyright Chrysler LLC. Used with permission.*

THE *NORSEMAN* AND THE HEMI'S IMPENDING DEMISE

When the Italian luxury liner *Andrea Doria* sank off the coast of Nantucket, Massachusetts, she took an irreplaceable piece of automotive history with her: Chrysler's *Norseman* concept car. Like the *K-310*, the *Norseman* had been built in Turin, Italy by Exner's favorite design house, Carrozzeria Ghia.

The *Norseman* embodied Exner's most ambitious design ideas to date. It featured aluminum body panels mounted to a frame that consisted of a pair of cantilevered steel arches that swung up and over the passenger compartment. The car took the hardtop concept a step further and removed the A pillar around the windshield so that the top relied solely on the C pillar around the rear window for all structural support. This design allowed Exner to install an electrically operated glass panel that covered the passenger compartment. The panel slid forward, leaving the rear seat open to the elements. Futuristic styling touches included concealed headlights (a feature that had briefly appeared on DeSoto models just before World War II ended civilian auto production) and concealed door handles. In many ways, this car presaged the 1966 Dodge Charger.

In a move that foretold the impending doom of the Hemi, the *Norseman* was powered by a "special advanced Chrysler engine," according to a Chrysler's press release of July 26, 1956. Instead of a mighty Hemi, Chrysler's records indicate the car was equipped with a 225-horsepower version of the 331-cubic-inch poly V-8.

Chrysler had introduced a smaller engine in 1955 that was much less expensive to produce than the complex Hemi. Chrysler called this engine the "poly" V-8, referring to the engine's twin-domed combustion-chamber design, which the company called "polyspherical." This design placed the intake and exhaust valves in line with each other, allowing engineers to use

Laden with features, the *Norseman* boasted a pillar-less windshield and a grille that allowed cooling air to enter the radiator with minimal flow disruption, reducing drag. It's interesting to note that this advanced concept vehicle did not have a Hemi engine, rather utilizing a conventional head design. Chrysler was already starting to step away from the Hemi powerplant in 1956. *Copyright Chrysler LLC. Used with permission.*

With its fastback design and extensive use of aluminum, the *Norseman* displayed a number of styling elements that would later find their way onto production vehicles. It had a 12-square-foot glass sunroof that slid forward, allowing rear seat passengers to work on their tan. *Copyright Chrysler LLC. Used with permission.*

just one rocker arm per cylinder. Even though the poly engine lacked hemispherical heads, it was no slouch. In stock two-barrel form, the 1956 model produced 225 horsepower; when equipped with an optional "Power Pak" (which consisted of a four-barrel carburetor and dual exhaust), the engine put out 250 horsepower, putting it dangerously close to Hemi territory. That the *Norseman* featured a poly rather than a Hemi V-8 didn't bode well for the long-term prospects for the expensive twin-rocker engine.

NOT-SO-SUBTLE EXCESS

Chrysler Corporation sales decreased dramatically for 1956; in fact, the U.S. auto industry as a whole contracted that year, to the tune of 2 million fewer units sold when compared to 1955. All the U.S. automakers were hurting, and all were willing to try something radical to turn sales around. Radical is just what the automotive stylists gave the public. And so, 1957 would be remembered as the year tailfins went over the top.

Virgil Exner was more than willing to go the mega-fin route in his designs, and he arguably designed exaggerated tailfins better than any other designer. In *Chrysler & Imperial 1946-1975*, Langworth quotes Virgil Exner Jr.:

> My father was a real staunch believer in fins. Like a lot of designers at the time, he was tremendously influenced by Italian designs—the Alfa BAT and the Cisitalia, for example. The idea of the fin was to get some poise to the rear of the cars, to get them off of the soft, rounded back-end look, to achieve lightness. To my dad, Italian design represented these characteristics, and [he] was good at achieving a sculptured effect, a very contemporary proportion.

The fins of the 1957 Chryslers even served a functional purpose—they had been designed in a wind tunnel to provide stability at speeds over 60 miles per hour. But as the decade wore on and manufacturers designed increasingly exaggerated tailfins, designers abandoned any pretext toward functionality.

For the first time, the 300 emblem was displayed on the side of the vehicle in 1957. The color scheme ensured that everyone who saw it knew that this was an American car. As if any other country would build something like this . . . .

Lower and more dramatic for 1957, the 300C looked ready for takeoff. From the massive front bumper to the swoopy tail fins, the muscular Chrysler beckoned to those longing a memorable experience.

With the use of smaller 14-inch wheels, Chrysler found that the 1957 300C tended to cook the brakes. This problem was addressed with the installation of brake cooling vents below the headlights, with ducting directing the air to the back of the brakes.

Few people believed such claims anyway. It didn't matter; the buying public loved the new jet-age look—at least initially.

No one doubted the functionality of another innovation Chrysler introduced for the 1957 model year: Torsion-Aire Ride, which was Chrysler's marketing name for its torsion-bar front suspension system. In theory these bars, which replaced traditional coil or leaf springs, absorbed forces generated by road irregularities more efficiently than the traditional designs. Torsion bars had long been used in European cars, and Packard had employed torsion bars in both the front and rear suspension systems on its 1955 models. (The Packard design even had a self-leveling system operated by electric motors.)

By 1957, Chrysler was in the thick of the fin battles, and the high-performance 300C was the ideal showcase.

Buyers in 1957 got a serious amount of metal for their moolah. With a price tag of $4,929 and a weight of 4,235 pounds, that worked out to just $1.16 per pound. That's real value!

Full-sized, the 1957 300C could haul a half-dozen people as well as their luggage with ease. The Hemi engine was enlarged, having grown to 392 cubic inches and able to generate 375 horsepower in the base engine, 390 horespower in the optional 10.0:1 compression Hemi.

Improved handling was the ostensible purpose of Chrysler's torsion-bar system; but its main functional advantage was that the system didn't occupy as much space as the tall coil-spring system and allowed Exner to design lower hoods. Plus the marketing name "Torsion-Aire Ride" gave Chrysler dealers another selling point—no small consideration in the tough auto market of 1957. The downside was that the bars had a tendency to fail, causing the front suspension to sag.

The three-speed Torqueflite automatic transmission, button-shifted as had been its predecessor, appeared in 1957. The new transmission was much better able to harness the power of the Hemi engine, which now had a horsepower rating that was almost as excessive as the height of the tailfins sprouting up all over Detroit.

Exner mounted his pronounced tail fins on the 300, now called the 300C. (The letter designation would remain a tradition throughout the car's lifespan, with each successive year advancing one letter up the alphabet.) He also gave the car a distinctive trapezoidal grille. For the first time, buyers could choose a convertible version of the 300, but the real news resided in the engine bay. Once again Chrysler's engineers had taken the boring bar to the Hemi, reaming the bores out to 4 inches. Combined with a stroke that was increased to 3.9 inches, the Hemi now measured 392 cubic inches. The twin four-barrel version of the engine mounted in the 300C produced 375 horsepower.

It cost a considerable sum, but the buyer of a 1957 300C never thought that he didn't get his money's worth. Rich leather covered the seats.

If 375 horsepower wasn't enough, Chrysler offered an optional engine and chassis package consisting of a full race cam, 10.0:1 compression pistons, manual steering, a manual transmission, heavy-duty clutch, and limited-slip differential. The end result was a 390-horsepower car capable of running 145 miles per hour or better. *Mechanix Illustrated's* Tom McCahill called it "the most hairy-chested, fire-eating land bomb ever conceived in Detroit."

The tailfins resonated with the general public and Chrysler Corporation had a spectacular year. DeSoto did its part to contribute to the corporate coffers, helped by the successful Adventurer, which sold almost double the number of units of the previous year. The engine now displaced 345 cubic inches and generated 345 horsepower. That might have been a bit less power than the "hairy-chested" 300C put out, but it was still a lot, and the Adventurer was quite a bit less expensive than the Chrysler muscle car. The DeSoto was not cheap, but a buyer could get an Adventurer coupe for $932 less than a similar 300C, and a convertible version cost a whopping $1,000 less than the convertible 300C.

Dodge still offered the D-500 package, which included a 325-cubic-inch Red Ram Hemi that, when equipped with optional dual-quad carburetors, cranked out 310 horsepower. Plymouth also joined the fray, offering a sporty model of its own: the Fury. This stylish car featured an engine—the Fury V-8, a 318-cubic-inch poly V-8 with two four-barrel carburetors, solid-lifter camshaft, and a 9.25:1 compression ratio—that generated 290 horsepower, nearly as much power as a Hemi for quite a bit less money. The Fury made Mopar muscle affordable for a much wider audience.

Full instrumentation faced the driver of a 300C, and rather numb power steering made maneuvering the large car a breeze.

Casting a big shadow, the 300C had a large influence on the performance car market, both in 1957 and beyond. The public's acceptance of a full-sized muscle car would be tapped again in the near future.

America's optimism in 1957 was limited only by the sky, and the 300C was the rolling embodiment of that optimism.

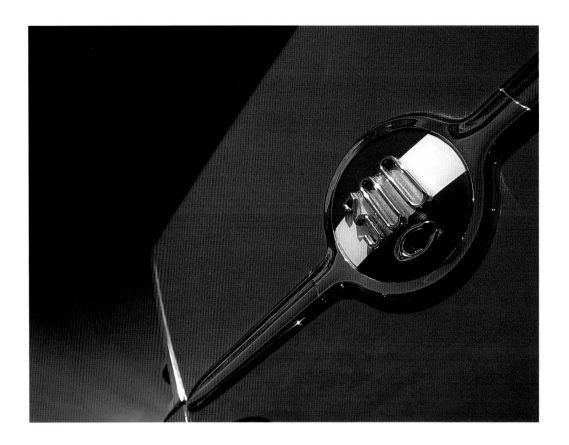

Dual four-barrel carburetors fed the 300C's 392-cubic-inch engine plenty of air and fuel, enough to generate 375-horsepower. That was more than enough to embarrass almost any other vehicle on the road.

"HAVE RESPECT FOR ITS POWER"

Because of the success of the 1957 models, Chrysler made very few changes for 1958. Like all manufacturers of the time, the company felt compelled to make at least minor trim changes for the new model year, so designers made haphazard tweaks here and there, compromising the purity of Exner's 1957 designs.

The most obvious change to the 300 muscle car was that it changed from the 300C to the 300D. Engineers increased the compression ratio of all Hemi engines to 10.0:1 and installed a different cam in the twin-quad 300D engine, translating to 380 horsepower in

It's said that the mark of a good designer is knowing when to lift the pen, and the styling staff responsible for the 300C had great instincts. The big Chrysler is as stylish today as it was in 1957.

Instead of two grill sections as in 1956, the 300C had a massive single grill. The Forward Look was in full bloom, giving the public fast looking, and fast moving, automobiles.

the base engine. This was up 5 horsepower from the previous year, but in exchange torque fell 15 lb-ft, from 450 to 435. This was more than enough to propel a stock 300D through the quarter-mile in 16 seconds flat at 84 miles per hour, and Norm Thatcher set a Class E record at Bonneville in 1958, getting his 300D up to 156.387 miles per hour. The last of the original Hemi muscle cars was a serious piece of equipment, and Chrysler's owner's manual issued a warning that owners should "have respect for its power and control its power with care."

ELECTROJECTION

The most intriguing option offered on the 1958 300D was the Electrojection electronic fuel injection system. This ambitious system, developed in conjunction with Bendix Corporation, relied on complicated pre-transistorized electronics that included an electronic modulator, an electronic fuel pump, and required the mounting of a 40-amp generator. This $640 option increased engine output by 10 horsepower; in other words, it equaled the optional engine and chassis package of the previous year.

Or at least it would have, had it worked. In this case, the reach of Chrysler's vaunted engineers exceeded their collective grasp. Vacuum tubes are not well-suited for life in the harsh environment of an engine compartment, and the Electrojection system proved a dismal failure. Chrysler sold just 16 of the 300Ds equipped with the expensive system, and ended up recalling all 16 cars and retrofitting them with dual four-barrel carburetors.

RACING BAN

Chrysler Corporation had already begun phasing out the Hemi in 1958; Dodge, Plymouth, and DeSoto performance models had begun using a new OHV V-8 design with a wedge-shaped combustion chamber, leaving just the 300D flagship with a Hemi engine.

By 1958 Chrysler had very little motivation to keep building the expensive Hemi. Racing success—the Hemi's *raison d'etre* since Tommy Thompson gave the Hemi its first NASCAR victory in the Motor City 250—no longer mattered. The expense of building this complicated and advanced engine had been justified in part by the promotional value of having Chrysler products win races around the country. But in 1957 Chrysler, along with all other U.S. automakers, abandoned the racetrack as a promotional venue.

As cars became more powerful and racing became more popular, people without driving talent began to emulate the exploits of their racing heroes on public streets. In many cases, these amateur "racers" competed in automobiles that were far too powerful for their skill levels. The results were spectacular wrecks worthy of inclusion in the goriest driver's education film. Voters hell-bent on saving the country's hot rodders from themselves began complaining about fast cars, street racing, and accidents, prompting the federal government to start grumbling about regulating the auto industry. In a preemptive measure, the Automobile Manufacturers Association (AMA), at the time the primary lobbying group for American auto manufacturers, instituted a voluntary ban on factory involvement in racing. Stripped of its promotional value, the expensive Hemi engine became virtually impossible to justify.

With the failure of the Electrojection system, Chrysler's mighty Hemi ended production on a somewhat low note. The carbureted versions were still the most powerful engines on the road—they wouldn't be surpassed in output for quite a few years to come—but they didn't dominate by the same margins as a few years earlier. Advanced engines from other manufacturers, and even from within Chrysler itself, were eliminating the need for building the complicated Hemi engine. After the 1958 model year Chrysler stopped offering Hemi engines. It seemed highly unlikely anyone would ever resurrect the design. ■

CHAPTER THREE

"WHAT WOULD IT TAKE TO BEAT THEM?"

"WHAT WOULD IT TAKE TO BEAT THEM?"

Chrysler engineers introduced the Hemi's replacement, the "wedge" B-block engine, in 1958, the last year of Hemi production. Because development money was too tight to design different engines for each division, as had been done with the Hemi, the company used this new engine across all divisions. To disguise the fact that the same mill powering a mighty Imperial also motivated a lowly Plymouth, each brand offered the new V-8 with slightly different displacements.

The new B engine would prove to be one of Chrysler's best and longest-lived engine designs. Distinguished by its deep-skirted block and front-mounted distributor, the power plant earned the nickname "wedge" because its combustion chambers were wedge-shaped rather than hemispherical or polyspherical. Wedge technology more closely adhered to the orthodox thinking of the day.

Page 150-151: The "W01"-code Dodge Coronet was one of the fastest cars ever produced by a large automobile manufacturer. Chrysler built 101 of these strictly-for-racing cars in 1965.

Page 152-153: (Main) Because the NHRA had outlawed the use of lightweight materials in the bodies of drag cars, Chrysler's race engineers used every means at their disposal to lighten the cars. The bodies were dipped in acid to remove metal and the inner headlights were removed. *(Inset)* The heart of the W01 Coronet and the R01 Belvedere Super Stock was the A990 Hemi race engine. This engine featured aluminum cylinder heads, while the stock Carter AFB carburetors were replaced with a pair of four-barrel Holleys.

To give the 1960 300F's huge trunk lid some visual drama, Chrysler dressed it up with a faux-spare tire outline. The taillights were pure period science-ficton.

Plymouth's highest-output version of the new engine, dubbed the Golden Commando by the division's marketing types, displaced 350 cubic inches and generated 305 horsepower. The top Dodge B-block displaced 361 cubic inches and produced 320 horsepower when topped by a pair of four-barrel carbs; the DeSoto version cranked out 345 horsepower from its 361 cubic inches of displacement.

Chrysler offered the star-crossed Bendix Electrojection electronic fuel injection system as an option on the B-block engine for 1958. With this system, the Plymouth version produced 315 horsepower, the Dodge version produced 333 horsepower, and the DeSoto produced 355 horsepower, but as with the Hemi, B-block fuel injection was an unmitigated disaster. All were recalled and replaced with dual four-barrel carburetors.

In 1959 Chrysler replaced the Hemi engine used in the 300D with a 413-cubic-inch version of the new wedge-head. Because the larger members of the B-block family gained their extra displacement in part through increased strokes, Chrysler dubbed the engine family the RB-series, "RB" standing for "raised block." Engineers tweaked the RB engine in the 300E to produce 380 horsepower, the same as the base version of the Hemi had the previous year, but sales fell to the lowest level yet and Chrysler sold fewer than 700 300Es. This was in part because of quality control problems that Chrysler's cars had been having since the 1957 redesign; but the deletion of the infamous Hemi from the engine bay also contributed to the car's failure in the marketplace. The new RB was a terrific engine, but it just didn't have the cachet of the Hemi.

Long, low, and luscious, the 300F oozed confidence, affluence, and the good life. It cost *just* $5,841 to be the envy of the neighborhood.

With its wide-opening doors and swivel seats, the 300F was the ideal stage for a lady in a skirt to make a dramatic yet demure entrance. Cables connected the doors and the seats, pivoting the seats as the doors shut, preventing any awkward moments.

For the buyer willing to ante up the money for a 300F, the result was a visual treat, inside and out. The lavish use of brightwork on the interior was simply an extension of the flamboyant exterior styling.

Chrysler's tradition of designating each successive year of 300 production with a letter would continue through 1965, by which time the company had worked its way to the letter "L."

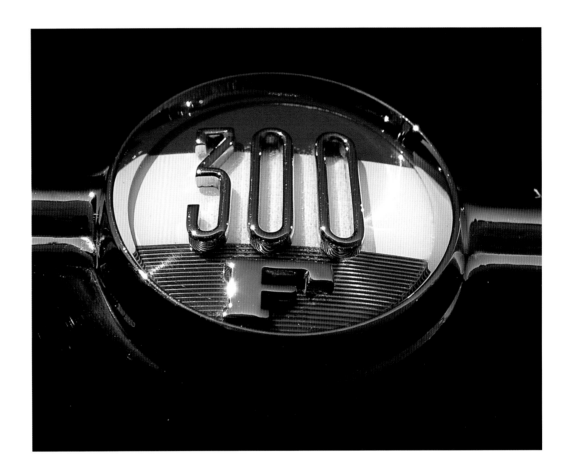

"WE DIDN'T KNOW DIDDLY ABOUT CRANKSHAFTS"

In a classic example of bad timing, the Hemi had just begun to come into prominence at the drag strip when Chrysler discontinued the engine. Racers were starting to understand how to tap the Hemi's potential. When racers first began using Hemis in their drag cars, they modified the engines in much the same ways they had modified their flatheads. They hadn't yet grasped the advantages of the Hemi's short stroke, a product of its oversquare bore and stroke ratio. As they had done with the flathead, they increased the stroke of the Hemi by building what they called "welded strokers," that is, by welding up extended-stroke crankshafts. In addition to

(Above): The graceful bumpers of the original C-300 had grown to massive chrome-plated railroad ties by 1961.

(Left): Had Virgil Exner not canted his 1960 fins to the side, their towering height would have impaired rearward visibility.

Two power levels were offered in the 300F, a standard engine rated at 375-horsepower, and an optional 400-horse mill. With 30-inch intake manifolds, the dual Carter AFB carburetors lived to pour large quantities of fuel into the 413-cubic-inch V-8.

lowering the engine's rev limit, the welded crankshafts often broke in competition. "At the time we didn't know diddly about crankshafts. . . . " Don Garlits admits in his autobiography.

When Don Garlits had his stroker engine grenade at a race in Biloxi, Mississippi, he made a discovery that would prove a major breakthrough in the sport of drag racing. In his autobiography Garlits recalls:

> I had no idea that a stock 392 Hemi would run that fast, because up until then we were used to running strokers. Because we couldn't afford to get another stroker motor, I did the only thing I could do. I got a stock 392-cubic-inch Hemi and put forged racing pistons in it with aluminum rods. Man, if that engine didn't have that car running like a rocket ship! It was a short stroke, so it picked up the boost, and it was a more efficient engine. We never ran a stroker again.

BACKDOOR RACING PROGRAMS

The most basic thing to understand about racing is that no one cheats; rather, every successful racer uses his or her resourcefulness to find ways to circumvent any and every rule that gets between him or her and victory. This has been the case since the first Mesolithic Nubian got in his occipital bun the notion that if he ran faster than the other Mesolithic Nubians, he could avoid becoming a human sacrifice.

Just as racers and race teams find resourceful ways to circumvent racing rules, so the manufacturers found ways to circumvent the AMA racing ban almost from the moment it

As the 1950s drew to a close, two-tone exterior paint schemes were very much in vogue; the 1959 Dodge Coronet Custom Royal cut a dramatic figure with its hues. The cat's-eye headlight brows added to the car's distinctive look.

Displacing 326-cubic inches, the Red Ram V-8 was rated at 255 horsepower at 4,400 rpm. It had 9.2:1 compression and used a Carter two-barrel carburetor.

While not as opulent as Chrysler's 300E, the 1959 Dodge D-500 was still plenty luxurious.

With a large automobile, stylists are able to create dramatic, sweeping lines and impressive silhouettes. The 1959 Dodge Coronet Custom Royal used a flowing C-pillar to visually lengthen the already long car.

It was no accident that the rear bodywork of the Dodge Coronet Lancer resembled a jet aircraft; in 1959, America was enamored with all things supersonic, and this Dodge looked only slightly slower than the sonic-boom generators high in the sky.

was instituted. Short of fielding factory race teams, the easiest way for the manufacturers to capitalize on the promotional benefits of racing was to provide top racers with under-the-table support. Don Garlits was one of the earliest recipients of such back-door sponsorship.

In 1958, the first full year of the racing ban, Garlits experimented with dragsters powered by Buick and Chevy engines. The folks at Chrysler had been following Garlits' on-track exploits and weren't thrilled to see him winning races in dragsters powered by small-block Chevrolet engines. Garlits writes:

> One day I got a call from Chrysler. Now, this was 1958. I had no relationship whatsoever with Chrysler. I was buying my engines in the junkyard. This fellow from Chrysler says, "We understand you ran a Chevy in your dragster."
> I said, "Well, yes, I did."
> He says, "Well, we don't like that. What's wrong with the Chrysler?"

When it came to raw performance, Dodge spent much of the 1950s lagging behind Chrysler and DeSoto; but by 1959 the division had begun to build a solid performance reputation.

Pity the poor car wash attendant who had to ensure all of the chrome was spot-free. The big Dodge D-500 saw a complete redesign for 1960.

Dodge's 1960 D-500 engine developed a stout 320-horsepower with the help of these cross ram intake manifolds and dual Carter AFB carburetors. While low rpm operation was adequate, the engine really lived for high revs.

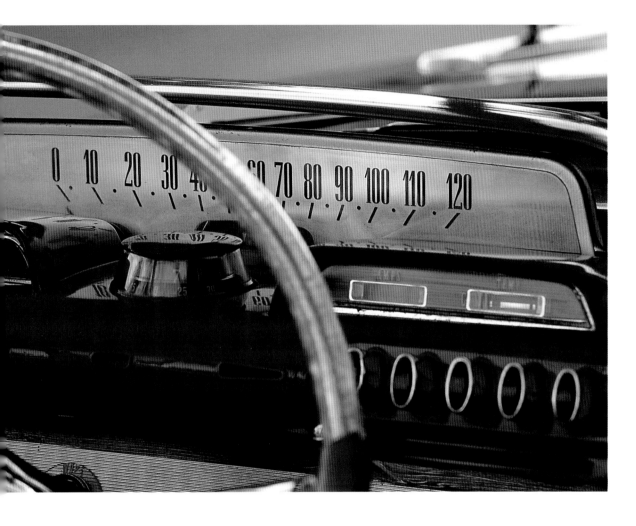

I said, "It's something we do. Ya know, we're always experimenting with different things to see what we can develop."

And he says to me, "We'd be more comfortable if you'd take that Chevy engine out and put a Hemi back in the car."

I said, "Well, I had a Buick in there before."

"But you can drop a Hemi in there, can't you?"

"Yeah," I said, "I can do that."

He finally says, "Then we'd be happy to supply you with some engines if you can do that."

Now, here's what they did from then on. There were a lot of these wealthy guys who bought Chrysler 300s and ran 'em hard and put 'em away wet. These were good customers of Chrysler, and the engines were under guarantee. These owners would beat these cars until something broke, like a rod bearing or something like that, and they'd drive them back to the dealer and shout, "Hey, my engine blew up!" Chrysler would drop a nice new engine—a new short-block assembly—into their cars, make them happy, and send the old

It didn't take a heck of a lot of throttle to transform the 383-cubic inch engine's power into a smoke screen. The bias ply tires of the era were good for this, and for keeping the chassis off the ground. They served little other purpose.

In 1960, few American automobiles could make as impressive an entrance as the Dodge Polara. It could even maintain that elegance when it was dusting just about every other car on the street.

engines to me. It was perfect for me, because we had to grind the cranks anyway, and the engines were in pretty good shape otherwise. So after that, I got all of the 392 Hemis I ever wanted from Chrysler.

With backdoor racing sponsorship, the requirements for competition once again began driving Chrysler engineers to improve the corporation's engines. Racing drove the development of other manufacturers too, AMA ban or not, and Chrysler needed to develop stronger engines to beat the competition in the marketplace as much as at the track.

There were other routes to improved performance besides bigger, stronger engines. One such route is to build lighter cars, and for the 1960 model year Chrysler introduced an innovation that allowed engineers to shed massive weight from the company's production cars: unit-body construction. Unit-body construction combines an integrated frame and body, instead of placing a separate body on top of a heavy, ladder-type frame. Chrysler wasn't the first automaker to use this method of construction. The Italian automaker Lancia first used the technology in 1922, and a handful of U.S. automakers, including Nash and Ford, had used it on some of their smaller cars. But Chrysler was the first automaker to build full-sized unit-body cars.

THE MAX WEDGE

With lighter unit-body cars in its lineup, Chrysler had unknowingly developed one half of the muscle-car formula. The other half was to develop a killer engine.

Lynn Townsend, who took over as president of Chrysler Corporation in 1961, after the board of directors ousted Tex Colbert, understood the relationship between racing success and sales success. Townsend had two teenage sons who were heavily involved in Detroit's street racing scene, which was centered around North Woodward Avenue. His sons' tales of hot Pontiacs beating Chryslers in impromptu Woodward Avenue drag races didn't sit well with Townsend. In late 1961 he ordered his engineers to develop an engine package that would make Chrysler cars once again the kings of the quarter-mile.

Since the Hemi was officially dead, this meant developing a hot rod version of the RB wedge engine. This engine, officially called the "Ramcharger" when mounted in the Dodge chassis and the "Golden Commando" when mounted in the Plymouth, but unofficially called the "Max Wedge," featured radical solid-lifter camshafts, large-port heads, and dual Carter AFB carburetors mounted atop a short ram intake manifold. In its most powerful form, this

Lynn Townsend. *Copyright Chrysler LLC. Used with permission.*

By 1962, Virgil Exner's relationship with Chrysler was nearing its end, and his stylistic creations were running increasingly counter to the public's taste. Chrysler made up for the unconventional designs with ever more powerful engines, such as the 413-cubic-inch mill in the Plymouth Belvedere shown here.

Generating 420 horsepower, the 413-cubic-inch Max Wedge V-8 was a flat-out racing engine. In a street car, it could prove to be a handful, but on the drag strip, it was brutal.

Exner-penned vehicles of this era had shapes and contours that left many people scratching their heads. But with uni-body construction and torsion-bar suspension, they were mechanically ahead of their time.

Exner placed the Belvedere name on the door of the 1962 sedan, above a chrome spear that highlighted the crease that ran the length of the front fender into the door.

Chrysler decided to reduce the size of their sedans, a move that worked out in favor of enthusiasts desiring a relatively lightweight body and a robust engine.

engine package produced 420 horsepower, making the new lightweight Chrysler products the belles of the drag strip ball. Pontiac had dominated drag racing in 1960. In 1961, Chevy's hot 409 had been the car to beat. In 1962, Mopars once again became the force to be reckoned with, and would remain so for a very long time.

Chrysler turned to Don Garlits to promote its hot new Max Wedge. In his autobiography, Garlits recalls his first experience with Chrysler's new drag racing weapon:

> In the fall of 1961, Chrysler had me come up to Detroit and showed me the 1962 Super Stock Dodge. They said they wanted me to have one. It had a 413 wedge-head engine and a cross-ram intake manifold—it was a trick car. . . . I took delivery of that car and it had a 3.31 rear axle in it. The first big race where all of the Super Stocks would be showing up was going to be at Green Valley, Texas. So my wife and I packed up our suitcases, threw them in the Dodge, and drove it to Green Valley! When we got to Texas, we went to a Dodge dealer and told them [to] put a 4.56 rear end in it. We drove it to the race, ran it, came back to the dealer, and had them put the 3.31 back in it. We drove all the way home to Tampa. It was really a stock car! And it was a fast car! It ran 13.5 or 13.6 at 112 miles per hour.

Bumpers were starting to no longer be something that you could actually bump into without damaging bodywork; instead, they were becoming merely stylistic elements.

On a drag strip, many competitors saw this view of the 413 Max Wedge. Equipped with the excellent A-727 3-speed Torqueflite automatic transmission, the car would hook up and hurl itself down the strip.

The Max Wedge package was available in two strengths on the 1964 Dodge 330; a 415-horsepower version that used an 11.0:1 compression, and a 425-horse setup that compressed the combustion chamber mixture at a 12.5:1 ratio. Better spring for the good gas.

Looking at the dashboard of the Dodge 330, it's clear that luxury really didn't fit into the vehicle's style. Utilitarian and proud of it.

Both variants of the 1964 426-ci Ramcharger V-8 used dual Carter AFB 3705S carburetors sitting atop a cross ram intake manifold.

On his drive to Texas, Garlits couldn't resist having a little fun with the Dodge. While he and Pat were cruising down the freeway at 80 miles per hour a hot rod Ford pulled up beside them. The driver of the Ford had no idea what Garlits was driving; up to that point, Chrysler had only built 13 Max Wedge-powered cars, and only a few Chrysler insiders knew what they were. The hot rodder just thought he was going to have some fun at the expense of some shmucks in a Dodge sedan. Garlits sped up to 90 and the Ford sped up to 90. Garlits sped up to 100 and the Ford sped up to 100. Garlits sped up to 120 and the Ford sped up to 120, which was extremely fast for a Ford. Garlits writes:

> I had the 3.31 gears, remember. The Ford was just about to run out of breath. The Dodge had those two big dual quads on a cross-ram, and when I stepped all the way down on it, I couldn't believe I had been only running about half throttle! When I put it to the wood, I looked in the mirror and saw two thick black tire marks on the highway behind me! With a 3.31 gear, that Dodge is leaving rubber at 120 miles per hour and we just drove away from that Ford. I bet that guy talks about that to this day to his grandchildren!

Garlits dabbled with Max Wedge-powered Super Stocker cars but focused most of his attention on his Hemi-powered Top Fuel dragsters, a sensible choice, since his Hemi-powered Swamp Rats continued to set speed record after speed record. Besides, Chrysler would soon have another project for him: developing a brand-new Hemi engine for Top Fuel racing.

The large scoop on top of the 1964 Dodge 330 Hemi's hood wasn't there for show. Lightweight, brutally fast, and very rare.

AN ELEPHANT IN A COCK FIGHT

Eternally the number three American automaker (except when the company had surpassed Ford for a brief period just after World War II), Chrysler was willing to do just about anything to increase its market share. And if racing success was the way to get it done, then the company's then-current batch of hot rod boys would do everything in their power to ensure racing success—even if it meant bringing an elephant to a cockfight. That elephant took the form of a reborn Hemi.

It wasn't that the Max Wedge was underpowered. In fact, the engine would continue to dominate America's drag strips for some time. The Max Wedge had been bored out to 426 cubic inches for 1963, just slipping under the National Hot Rod Association (NHRA) limit of 427.2 cubic inches for Super Stock engines. Its parts list summarized the state of push-rod V-8 engineering art: double-row timing chain, one-piece short-ram aluminum intake manifold topped by a pair of four-barrel carburetors, header-type exhaust manifold, high-capacity fuel pump, dual-point distributor, forged-aluminum pistons, Magnafluxed connecting rods, high-strength valve spring retainers, smaller crankshaft pulley (to limit belt speeds), and heavy-duty clutch with an aluminum clutch housing. It even had a deep-sump oil pan that was baffled to prevent oil from sloshing away from the sump when the car inevitably wheelied off the starting line. With an optional 13.5:1 compression ratio, the engine produced 425 horsepower.

In order to transfer some of the Hemi's cachet to the Max Wedge, Chrysler tried to get top drag racers to abandon the Hemis and switch to the RB engines. Don Garlits remembers one such attempt:

> In 1962, the NHRA must have had some clout with Dodge, because Frank Wylie called me up and he said, "We want you to build a gas dragster with the wedge motor and race it at the U.S. Nationals. We don't want you to run the 392 because we don't make it anymore.

Garlits didn't have much luck with the wedge and switched back to the Hemi soon after. But his lack of success had more to do with his long-running feud with the NHRA than with any of the engine's deficiencies. Other racers had terrific success with the Max Wedge, or at least other drag racers had success.

The problem was that the Max Wedge couldn't win on NASCAR's oval tracks. The engines performed well in short bursts, such as when being run flat-out on a quarter-mile drag strip, but the shape of the combustion chamber limited the size of intake and exhaust valves that Chrysler engineers could install. The wedge design also provided a less-than-optimum path for the fuel charge to enter the chamber, and for exhaust gasses to leave the chamber. While the wedge engine was a fantastic street engine and more than adequate for most forms of drag racing, these inherent design drawbacks resulted in diminished performance at the high rpm levels required for a successful NASCAR engine.

Lynn Townsend knew that to compete in an increasingly youth-oriented market, Chrysler would have to succeed in NASCAR as well as in drag racing. Townsend sought advice on the lack of NASCAR success from a group of engineers that included Tom Hoover, who was the engineering coordinator for Chrysler's race program at the time. Hoover, a Pennsylvania native who had grown up in a Mopar family—his father had worked in a Chrysler dealership—was also involved with the Ram Chargers, a group of Chrysler engineers who spent their spare time drag racing, both at the track and on Woodward Avenue. A long-time fan of the Hemi engine, Hoover's personal ride was a 1959 Plymouth in which he'd transplanted a 392 Hemi.

In an August 2005 interview in *Hot Rod* magazine, Hoover recalls getting the approval to develop a new Hemi:

> After the 1963 Daytona 500, won by Pontiacs, Mr. Townsend passed down the word: "What would it take to beat them and win the 1964 Daytona 500?" In response, the engineering vice president, a man named Bob Rodger, called a group of four or five of us together and we told him the best thing would be to go with the design we had experienced the greatest power with, and that was the Hemi. The outcome of all that was that in April of 1963 we were given the green light to fit Hemi heads onto the wedge block. And we did, very successfully.

Dodge's 1964 Hemi-powered drag racing sedans were stripped of the original rear bench seats. Two lightweight bucket seats replaced the front seat.

THE SECOND COMING OF THE HEMI

Thus in April 1963 Hoover's team was given the mandate of developing an engine that could win one of the world's most prestigious automobile races. And they had less than 10 months to get the job done. Such a schedule should have been impossible, but Hoover and his crew were exceptionally dedicated and resourceful. The A-864 Race Engine Program they embarked upon would prove to be one of the most extraordinary, ambitious, and successful engine development programs in the history of the U.S. auto industry.

Rolling out of the garage, looking for a fight, a 1964 Dodge Lightweight Hemi was a scary fast car. In an effort to lighten the car, Dodge removed the high-beam headlights.

A handful of factory lightweight cars were built, with the body dipped in acid to eat away at the metal. It counteracted the weight of the huge engine.

But the hot rod boys in Chrysler engineering were one step ahead of Townsend. An advance engine design group headed by Bob Dent had already begun developing hemispherical heads for the Max Wedge. Frank Bialk, the lead designer of the advance engine group, had begun drawing up plans several weeks before getting the official green light.

In the 426 Max Wedge block, Bialk and the rest of Dent's team had terrific raw material with which to work. The crankshaft-support structure of the old 392 Hemi had been a weak point of the design, and the deep-skirted RB engine had a much stronger crankshaft mounting design. "We could put unbelievable cylinder pressure on it and the crankshaft stays where it is supposed to be," Hoover told *Hot Rod*. "It doesn't get pushed out onto the street where you have to drive over it." To further strengthen the bottom end of the new engine, Bialk designed main bearing caps held in place by cross bolts that ran through the engine block. In this design, the engine block itself bears some of the tremendous loads to which the crankshaft would be subjected.

Getting heat into a drag tire is necessary to soften up the compound and ensure maximum grip. Post sedans tended to have rigid structures, aiding in getting the power down equally to both tires.

The burnout is always a crowd favorite. A car coming out of the water box with a plume of smoke in its wake, on its way to lunging 1,320-feet is always a welcome sight.

When the 1964 race Hemi was released, it was equipped with a dual quad cross ram intake manifold similar to the one used on the Max Wedge engine. Both Holley (shown) and Carter carburetors were used.

Early on, the team made the decision to retain the original Hemi's valve angle. This created challenges for the team when it came to developing a rocker arm system. One developmental goal for the new Hemi heads was that the rocker arms had no more rotational inertia than the system used in the smaller 392 Hemis. This lack of rotational inertia was what allowed racers like Garlits and Keith Black to reliably run their engines up to 7,500 rpm. If the two valves were equidistant, as on the original engine, the exhaust rocker arm would be so long that it would limit engine rpm.

It also presented a packaging problem. A head with such long rocker arms would not fit in the engine bay of the intended recipients of the new Hemi, the corporation's lightweight B-body cars. The engines wouldn't fit because of the method Chrysler used to assemble its unit-body cars. Chrysler dropped the bodies down over the engines during the assembly process, and if Hoover's team didn't narrow the rocker covers, the engine wouldn't fit between the fender wells.

Hoover's solution was to tilt the entire head inward, toward the intake manifold, simultaneously allowing the use of shorter exhaust rocker shafts while allowing the engine to fit in the B-body cars. This resulted in slicing off a small section of the hemispherical combustion chamber, meaning that the 426 Hemi has a combustion chamber that is not completely hemispherical, which is why some people refer to the 426 as a "semi-Hemi." While this slicing of the combustion chamber did result in an extremely slight loss in thermodynamic efficiency, this was more than compensated for by an increased redline. Any performance loss would remain in the realm of the theoretical, a matter of more importance to armchair commandos than it would be to anyone actually racing a Hemi-powered car.

Designing head bolts that would be strong enough to handle the tremendous pressure produced in the hemispherical combustion chambers proved another challenge. The wedge design used a five-bolt head-bolt pattern, as opposed to the four-bolt pattern used on the original Hemis. The problem was that when the heads were tilted inboard, there was no room for the extra bolt. Bialk's solution was to run the fifth bolt up from underneath the engine rather than down through the head itself. This system would flummox many a dealer mechanic when a street version of the engine became available, but the engine was never designed to be driven on the street, much less worked on by some hack over at the local Dodge shop.

The team developed two separate intake systems: a dual-quad system for drag racing and a single-four-barrel system for stock car racing. NASCAR regulations disallowed multiple carburetors, so the NASCAR manifold used a dual-plane design and featured a single Holley four-barrel carb. The drag racing manifold used a cross-ram design in which the four-barrel Carter carbs fed the four cylinders on the opposite side of the engine. Knowing how much weight the complicated Hemi heads would add to the already-heavy 426 RB engine, Chrysler cast both manifolds from aluminum.

There were no external markings denoting that this 1964 Dodge was packing a Hemi.

THE SUM OF ITS PARTS

No mass-produced engine had ever been assembled from such high-end components as was the 426 Hemi, and no mass-produced engine since has contained such quality components. Forged rods connected the forged aluminum pistons to the crankshaft, which was either forged from SAE 4340 high-strength alloy steel (for stock car racing) or SAE 1046 carbon steel (for drag racing). The crankshafts were heat treated, machined, and shot-peened, then hardened through a nitride immersion process called Tufftride.

The team developed two camshaft profiles, one for drag racing and another for stock car racing. Both versions worked against forged steel mechanical lifters with brazed-on iron facing. These pushed heavy-duty steel tubing pushrods against hardened forged-steel rocker shafts. The rockers featured full-length steel-backed bronze bushings and pressed-in hardened steel inserts where they contacted the pushrods. The gigantic valves (2.25-inch intake and 1.94-inch exhaust) required two springs apiece to operate properly. The exhaust valves opened into 2-inch steel tubular headers.

As soon as the Hemi head and block designs were finalized, Chrysler's foundry in Indianapolis began casting the engine blocks. Chrysler contracted the Campbell, Wyant and

This is the only non-post Hemi Dodge Super Stock built. The remaining cars, and there were few, were post sedans, meaning they had a B-pillar. The original buyer ordered a 426 Max Wedge, but because the engine had gone out of production, the factory installed a race Hemi instead.

Canon Foundry Company of Muskogee, Michigan, to begin casting the cylinder heads. Once the cylinder blocks and heads were cast at their respective foundries, they were shipped to Chrysler's Trenton, Michigan, engine plant for machining.

From there the early race engines were shipped to Chrysler's engine labs in Highland Park, where engineers would assemble them by hand. (When the street Hemi came out, final assembly took place at Chrysler's engine assembly plant in Marysville, Michigan.) Engineers in the Highland Park lab checked for cracks in the aluminum pistons and steel blocks, cranks, rods, and heads.

The entire assembly process took about 80 hours per engine, most of which was consumed by testing the components to make sure that they were within the specified tolerances. The first engine was assembled in the first week of December 1963, just two months before the tech inspection for the Daytona race.

A MODEST 425 HORSEPOWER

Chrysler rated the new Hemi at 425 horsepower, the same rating given to its Max Wedge predecessor. Everyone assumed that the artificially low power rating was the result of an effort on Chrysler's part to mask the true potential of its radical new engine, but in reality the low rating was the result of a much less nefarious cause. In his book *Hemi: History of the Chrysler V-8 Engine and Hemi-Powered Muscle Cars* (Motorbooks, 1991), author Anthony Young quotes Steve Baker, a Chrysler engineer who worked on assembling the Hemi engines in the Chrysler lab:

> "At the time," Baker remembers, "[the engine assembly lab] had a 400-horsepower Amplidyne dynamometer. Well, we knew we had a hell of a lot more horsepower. There were several of us there—the operator, myself, and the department manager, Ev Moeller. So we slide-ruled the observed power. We got 400 horsepower around 4,800 rpm. There was a possibility that we were going to break the dyno. Moeller was in charge and said to go ahead. He would take responsibility so the operator wouldn't get into trouble for damaging equipment. As I remember, we got up to more than 425 horsepower the very first run we made with the engine—and the dyno didn't break. Everyone was pretty pleased with that.

Even though everyone knew the engine produced far more than 425 horsepower, there wasn't time to get the equipment necessary to produce the true horsepower figures. Later field tests showed actual output to be closer to 565 horsepower, but the 425 number stuck with the Hemi throughout its production lifespan. It really didn't matter anyway—the Hemi was never designed to win in magazine spec-sheet contests; it was designed to win races.

WEAPON OF NASCAR DESTRUCTION

In the weeks remaining before the Daytona 500, the crew at the Highland Park lab worked insane hours to prepare the engines. They ran the dynamometers 24 hours a day, curing the problems that cropped up with the new engine. And there were quite a few problems to cure, the most serious involving engine failures caused by cracking in the right side of the block. On January 28, 1964, just days before the February 4 prerace inspection at Daytona, Willem L. Weertman, Chrysler's manager of engine design, flew to Indiana to try to solve the problem. Through trial and error Weertman and his crew arrived at a process in which the freshly cast blocks were placed in a large furnace and reheated to 1,200 degrees Fahrenheit to relieve any internal stress within the metal. Then the temperature in the oven was slowly lowered before the block was removed from the furnace.

These new blocks were shipped straight to Trenton for machining, then to the Highland Park lab for assembly. Weertman and his crew had accomplished a superhuman feat in preparing a durable engine block in such a short time, but the blocks didn't leave the foundry until

February 3, which meant Chrysler wasn't able to ship them to the race teams for installation and testing prior to the Daytona tech inspection and preliminary races. Instead they shipped engines with the faulty block design and hoped they would hold up until the more durable engines were ready.

Meanwhile the development team mounted one of the new Hemis in a stock car racing chassis and headed to the Goodyear track at San Angelo, Texas. The car hit 180 miles per hour its first time out. This presented a dilemma for Chrysler. Townsend wanted to win the 500, but no one wanted the company's cars to be so dominant that they attracted the attention of the NASCAR establishment. Chrysler eventually intended to produce enough examples of the new engine to homologate it for NASCAR racing, but there was no way that would be possible in the time frame specified by NASCAR. If the cars were too dominant, the other manufacturers would squawk, forcing NASCAR to declare the Chrysler offerings illegal for competition.

So Chrysler's racing department ordered the drivers not to do any wide-open laps during testing. This was in part because drivers were still using the original flawed blocks, but also in part to keep NASCAR officials from scrutinizing the new engine too closely. Drivers were ordered to lap the track at around the same speed as the Fords, which was roughly 170 miles per hour. Mostly this sand-bagging tactic worked, though a few drivers couldn't resist showing off the new engine's potential; Paul Goldsmith qualified with an average two-lap speed of 174.91 miles per hour, a new track record, and Lee Petty's son, a dark-haired young lad named Richard, qualified with an average speed of 174.418 miles per hour.

When the qualifying races began, the new Hemi-powered Chryslers broke track record after track record. They also broke a block or two, but the revised blocks were on their way and would make it to the race teams just in time for the February 23 race. Hemi-powered Mopars took all three spots on that year's Daytona 500 podium, with Richard Petty taking top honors.

Townsend was so thrilled with the results at Daytona that he wanted to develop an engine to race in the Indianapolis 500, but he cooled his jets after learning that it would cost approximately $7 million and even then the chances of winning would be slim.

As could be expected from the Daytona results, Petty won the 1964 Grand National championship. Hemi-powered cars won 26 Grand National races that year, humiliating Chrysler's competition in the process. The inevitable result of this was that the cars attracted the unwanted attention that Chrysler's race managers had feared.

WOODWARD AVENUE PRODUCT PLANNING GARAGE

By getting Chrysler Corporation involved in racing in such an overt fashion, Townsend was flaunting the AMA racing ban, and putting the company at risk of retribution. Chrysler needed to tone down its racing activities, so it moved its racing program to a site away from Highland Park.

Richard Petty on his way to his first Daytona 500 victory. The year is 1964, Petty's Number 43 Plymouth is powered by a 426 Hemi, and the second- (Jimmy Pardue) and third-place (Paul Goldsmith) finishers are also coasting on Hemi horsepower. And NASCAR is about to outlaw Chrysler's world-beating engine. *RacingOne/Getty Images*

Chrysler's corporate headquarters did not provide the ideal environment for race development. The engine lab in Highland Park couldn't be commandeered indefinitely for race engine development, and it allowed for too much corporate interference. So Tom Hoover found an abandoned Pontiac dealership on Woodward Avenue and the racing department relocated there. This facility became the epicenter for the development of Hemi-powered race cars.

The Woodward Avenue product planning garage proved an ideal location, because Chrysler's Ram Chargers intended to take the new engine drag racing. They could develop products and install them during the day, then go out and test them in Woodward Avenue street races in the evening.

THE DEFINITION OF "PRODUCTION CAR"

In order to homologate the Hemi for NASCAR, Chrysler had to build a certain number of production cars with the engine, though what that actual number was seemed to be something along the line of we'll-know-it-when-we-see-it. This ambiguity gave NASCAR tighter control over the on-track action. If the sanctioning body wanted a car to compete, then the manufacturer had built enough examples; if a car proved too dominant and detracted from the close racing that put asses in the bleachers, then that car may well not have been built in a large-enough quantity.

Of course the actual number of production cars Chrysler intended to build with Hemi engines was fairly concrete, if you define production cars as "street legal passenger cars": zero. The engine had not been developed with the requirements of street-legal passenger cars in mind. Instead, Chrysler intended to build a number of engines and complete cars for drag racing use only. In other words, it planned to build drag cars to homologate its stock cars. In a paper that he presented to the SAE in 1966, Weertman explained the plan:

> Immediately following the introduction of the engine, a production run of several
> hundred drag racing engines and cars were planned to be built. The production
> of the several hundred drag engines would be completed by the end of the 1964
> model year. Another production run of several hundred drag engines was made
> for the 1965 model year automobiles, with a considerable weight decrease for the
> engines obtained by use of aluminum and magnesium components.

The 1964 Hemi cars were not created on a factory assembly line, but rather were shipped to Automotive Conversions, a company that manufactured ambulances and limousines.

There they were converted to stock-looking drag racing cars. The only visual clues as to what madness lurked beneath their hoods were shovel-like hood scoops that funneled huge amounts of fresh air to the hungry pair of four-barrel carburetors feeding the engines.

The 1964 drag cars stretched any definition of "production car" beyond the breaking point. Standard equipment included a Sure-Grip limited slip differential housing 4.56:1 gears, though the car could be ordered with optional gear sets ranging from 2.93:1 to 5.38:1. A compression ratio of 12.5:1 insured that owners couldn't pull up to their corner gas station and fill the tank with whatever octane happened to be available, but the cars were never meant to be driven anywhere near the corner gas station. The rear window was replaced with 0.08-inch tempered glass and window winders were eliminated to save weight. Even the insulating backing on the carpet was eliminated in the name of saving weight. These cars were meant for racing use only, a fact made clear in Dodge's promotional literature:

> The Hemi-Charger [initially Dodge called the Hemi engines in its cars "Hemi-
> Chargers"] engine is designed for use in supervised acceleration trials and other
> racing and performance competition. It is not recommended for everyday

driving because of the compromise of all-around characteristics which must be made for this type of vehicle. In view of its intended use this vehicle is sold "As Is" and the provisions of Chrysler Corporation's manufacturer's passenger car warranty or any other warranty expressed or implied do not apply.

The booklet went on to list the available racing components, a list that that read like a manifesto of the state of drag racing technology: aluminum fenders, hoods, dust shields, front bumpers, bumper-support brackets, and doors. Plexiglass was available to replace the glass in the doors and front vent windows. Even without the optional drag racing equipment, with the right person behind the wheel, each of the 1964 Hemis that Chrysler unleashed on the public was capable of breaking into the 11-second quarter-mile bracket right out of the box. Suffice to say, these Dodges and Plymouths were some of the quickest cars ever produced.

Not every budding drag racer could buy the new Chrysler Hemis, either, which further stretched the definition of "passenger car." Rather, the Woodward Avenue race shop provided cars to carefully screened racers, drivers, and teams, i.e., people with the skills to handle the potent machines and proven performance records that ensured the maximum publicity for Chrysler. The shop gave cars to proven racers like Don Garlits, while most racers couldn't buy a Hemi for any amount of money.

While the number of 1964 Hemis that found their way to the street is so low as to be almost negative, a few resourceful enthusiasts figured out how to acquire examples of the mythical beasts. Lynn Ferguson, a casual drag racer from St. John, Michigan, was one such enthusiast. Tired of losing in his 1951 Ford six-cylinder, Ferguson saved up and ordered a car he knew would win races: a Super Stock Dodge 440 with a 426-cubic-inch Max Wedge in Stage III trim. After four months of waiting, he learned that Chrysler had ceased production of Max Wedge engines, but they would be replaced by another engine.

Six weeks later he plunked down $3,820.25 cash and found himself the proud owner of one of the rarest American performance cars ever built. Other than the upside down shovel on the hood, one of the few clues as to the car's true nature was a sticker inside the glove compartment that read: "Notice. This car is equipped with a 426 cu. in. engine (and other special equipment). This car is intended for use in supervised acceleration trials and is not for highway or general passenger car use."

RACING ENGINE PROGRAM A-990

If the regular Hemi wasn't special enough, the madmen at the Woodward Avenue garage developed an even more special version for 1965. Chrysler dealers announced the coming of this new drag racing package on November 11, 1964. The cars, a Plymouth Belvedere given the production code "R01" and a Dodge Coronet, the "W01," looked like any other Hemi Super Stock car, except that the inner headlights were deleted on the Dodge. (Since the Plymouth had only two headlights to start with, this modification was unnecessary.)

While the cars looked stock, their looks deceived. Because the lightweight 1964 Hemis had been so dominant, the National Hot Rod Association (NHRA) outlawed the use of aluminum body parts and plexiglass windows for 1965. To get around this, Chrysler made the bodies of the cars from lightweight steel that was 40 percent thinner than the steel used on the standard production cars. While Chrysler hasn't officially admitted this, the perpetrators responsible have since admitted that the cars' body parts had been acid-dipped to make them lighter.

But what separated these 1965 cars from their 1964 counterparts more than anything was their Hemi engines. The 1965 powerplant, internally referred to as the A-990 Race Engine, featured a redesigned camshaft and a few other tweaks. But its main innovation was its use of lightweight materials. Bill Weertman and his crew of miscreants cast the cylinder heads for the A-990 from aluminum, and also used aluminum alloy for the water pump housing, oil pump housing and cover, water outlet, and alternator brackets. They used magnesium for the intake manifold, and replaced the Carter AFB carburetors with a pair of Holley four-barrel units.

The A-990-equipped cars came ready-to-race as delivered from the factory, and owners couldn't load them up with options like heaters, air conditioners, and radios. The only choice a buyer could make was whether to select an automatic transmission or a four-speed manual transmission. The A-833 four-speed manual transmission had become available as an option in 1964, marking the first time a Hemi had ever been available with a four-on-the-floor transmission. Previous choices had either been an automatic slush box or a three-on-the-tree manual. For 1965, the A-833 resided inside an aluminum housing when it backed a Hemi engine, rather than the heavy steel housing it featured in more pedestrian applications.

The A727B Torqueflite transmission was a new option for 1965. The 727 would prove to be one of the best transmissions of the classic muscle-car era and would remain in production for many years. It is still a favorite of hot rodders today because of its reliability and durability. The A727B, the heavy-duty version that backed a Hemi engine, was modified for manual shifting and the valve bodies were reversed, so that the shifting pattern was the opposite of what it was in normal use. This allows drag racers to slam through the gears without worrying about hitting neutral, or worse yet, reverse. The A727B differed from the proletariat 727 in that it featured five discs instead of four to better cope with the Hemi's unbelievable power output.

Sticker price for the W01, given the cumbersome marketing name "Coronet Hemi-Charger," was $4,717 and the sticker for the R01, called the "Belvedere Super Stock," was $4,671. It's hard to imagine what might have accounted for the $46 price discrepancy in these otherwise identical cars, other than the fact that "Dodge" was a more prestigious nameplate than "Plymouth." As if that mattered on the racetrack . . .

Chrysler built 101 examples of each of these cars, with the Plymouth's production run ending in late 1964 and Dodge's in early 1965. They were more widely available than had been the Hemis of the previous year. You no longer had to be a connected racer to buy a Hemi, though most still went to professional teams and drivers. They had to build at least 100 examples of each car to satisfy the NHRA's minimum requirement to make a car legal for the Super Stock class. They also built the cars in an attempt to homologate the Hemi for NASCAR racing, but Bill France and company didn't buy it.

To facilitate engine access, many racers converted the 1964 Plymouth Belvedere race car's hood from a normal hinge operation to a lift-off hood.

NASCAR RETALIATES

In 1964, Chrysler had gone over the top with the Hemi, building an engine that was so dominant that it threatened to turn the Grand National series into the Hemi cup. At the same time, Henry Ford II—the Deuce—had wanted to win a NASCAR championship every bit as much as had Lynn Townsend, and the Deuce did not take kindly to having the lowly Chryslers humiliate his Fords for an entire year. In retaliation, Ford developed the Cammer engine, a 427-cubic-inch powerplant with a camshaft perched above each cylinder head.

Chrysler responded with the A-925 engine program. Chrysler figured that if one overhead cam was good, two would be better, and the A-925 was a double-overhead-cam design. Not only that, it operated four valves per cylinder instead of two, technically making it a pent-roof design rather than a hemispherical design, but since it was a Chrysler, everyone still called it a Hemi. Chrysler built a prototype but never actually ran the engine. The purpose of the A-925 was intimidation. Bob Rarey, Chrysler's chief engine designer at the time, tells the story as quoted in Anthony Young's *Hemi*:

> Ford went down to Daytona for 1965 with their racing engine [the Cammer] . . . which wasn't a hemi, exactly, but was darned near, I guess. They said they wanted to race *that* against us. Ronnie Householder went in to Bill France and said, "Hey, look fellows, if you run that Ford engine, we're running this engine." He takes the cover off it and shows the four-valve Hemi. This engine had a 16-branch manifold. It was unbelievable. France just said, "As of now, the Ford engine isn't running and neither is *that*."

In order to fit wide rear tires without modifying the body, the inner wheel wells were often "tubbed"—new inner wheel wells were constructed, filling up a considerable amount of trunk space.

If Householder had intended to scare Bill France, he succeeded too well. France banned more than just the A-925; he also banned Chrysler's Hemi.

NASCAR's banishment of the Hemi from its superspeedways so angered Chrysler that it pulled all factory NASCAR-racing support for the 1965 season. In its attempt to avoid turning the Grand National series into the Chrysler Cup, NASCAR had inadvertently turned it into the Ford Cup, since Ford was the only factory still actively competing in the series.

IDLE HANDS

Chrysler's withdrawal from NASCAR competition forced drivers to find something else to do for an entire season. It also left the mad geniuses at the Woodward Avenue garage with far too much time on their hands. They needed to find some worthy activity in which they could occupy NASCAR types like Richard Petty, Cotton Owens, and David Pearson.

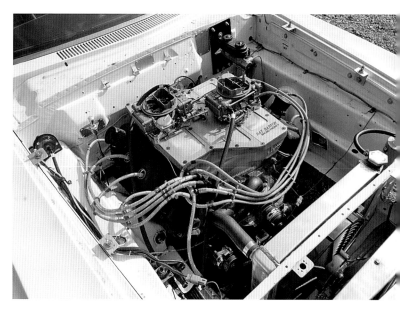

If the carburetor barrels were any larger, small animals would be at risk. A race-ready 426 Hemi is a violent machine.

By this time the A/Factory Experimental (A/FX) class had superseded the Super Stock class as the premiere drag racing class (the A/FX class would eventually morph into the funny car class). This new class would prove a fertile ground for the talents of Chrysler's racing engineers, tuners, and drivers.

For 1965 Ford planned to campaign Mustangs and Comets powered by the Cammer engine. The A/FX rules allowed wheelbases to be decreased by up to 2 percent to put more weight on the rear tires, allowing them to hook up better off the line, but Ford openly flaunted that rule, so the Woodward Avenue crew decided to follow suit. They took six W01 and five R01 cars and moved the axles forward 15 inches. To accomplish this, engineers removed a 15-inch section of the rear floor pan and moved the rear end forward. A 15-inch flat pan was riveted over the area previously occupied by the rear axle. The crew modified the rear fenders to move the wheel arches ahead to the new location of the wheels.

To compensate, the front wheels were moved forward 10 inches. To accomplish this, engineers fabricated new front side-members and removed the crossmember that supported the upper control arms and torsion bar springs. They fabricated a new crossmember and mounted it at the very front of the car, right below and just behind the front bumper. Since this crossmember normally supported the Hemi engine, new motor mounts had to be devised. Moving the front end assembly proved a much more complicated job than moving the rear assembly, because it required fabricating longer steering rods and torsion springs. Almost every suspension component had to be hand-fabricated, and all were made from the strongest material at the shop's disposal.

Since lighter materials were allowed in the A/FX class, these cars used lightweight fiberglass for the radically scooped hood, doors, deck lid, front bumpers, instrument panel, and front fenders (which had the wheel openings moved forward to the very front of the car). The rest of the body was acid-dipped to remove excess weight. This process caused problems later on.

Dave Strickler ran this 1965 A/FX Dodge Coronet 330 on drag strips across the country. For better weight transfer during acceleration, the rear axle was moved forward 15 inches, while the front axle was moved forward 10 inches, resulting in a 110-inch wheelbase.

These cars were shipped in body-in-white form, which means that they weren't painted, but rather just dipped in a light coat of primer, and it was up to the racing teams that got the cars to paint them with their own racing livery. The problem was that the acid dipping must have left a thin residue of acid on the bodies. This kept eating away at the paint and sheet metal over the entire lifespan of the cars, forcing teams to repaint their cars multiple times.

Amblewagon, an ambulance-building company in Troy, Michigan, handled final assembly of the cars. Some cars were ready for the start of the 1965 season, but not all of them were, and cars trickled out of Amblewagon throughout the winter and into the early spring.

Topped by eight velocity stacks, the 426-cubic-inch race Hemi in Dave Strickler's 1965 Coronet was a consistent monster, able to crank out 10-second runs all day long.

These cars were shipped to a carefully selected group of top racers. Ronnie Sox, Tom Grove, Butch Leal, Forrest Pitcock, and Al Exstrand received the Plymouths; Dick Landy, Jim Thornton, Roger Lindamood, Bob Harrop, Dave Strickland, and Bud Faubel received the Dodges. In addition, Bill Flynn from New Haven, Connecticut, had his W01 converted to A/FX specifications, resulting in a total of 12 cars built (13, if you consider a developmental mule car that also competed in 1965, but that car appears to have been dismantled after the 1965 Winternationals in Pomona, California).

The American Hot Rod Association's (AHRA) rules allowed these altered wheelbase cars to compete in its Ultra Stock (U/S) class, but the NHRA took umbrage at Chrysler's flaunting the organization's two-percent rule regarding the relocation of the rear axle and banned the cars from its A/FX class. As a result, the Woodward Avenue garage built four cars to the same specifications as the altered-wheelbase cars, except that the axle was only moved ahead a legal two-percent. These are referred to as the "legal two-percent cars."

Wherever the altered wheelbase cars were allowed to compete, they dominated the competition and broke all existing records. On April 24, 1965, Ronnie Sox of the fabled Sox & Martin team ran a 9.98 quarter-mile at the drag strip in York, Pennsylvania, a new record for a stock-bodied automobile without forced induction. Sox used a new Hilborn fuel injection system developed by Chrysler's Woodward Avenue race team to set his record time. ■

CHAPTER FOUR

"THE HOTTEST HUNK OF IRON TO HIT THE STREETS"

"THE HOTTEST HUNK OF IRON TO HIT THE STREETS"

In banning the Hemi from NASCAR's superspeedways, Bill France inadvertently spurred the development of the street Hemi. Chrysler still wanted to race in the Grand National series, and the only way that would happen would be for the company to offer a version of its Hemi race engine as a regular production option in its passenger cars.

Right from the start of the A-864 Race Engine Program, Chrysler's engineers looked into ways of reducing the staggering production costs of the Hemi, in order to make the engine viable in a street-legal vehicle. There were no easy ways to avoid the expensive manufacturing costs while still producing an engine that was as reliable as it was powerful. If anything, developing a civilian version for the street would add to the astronomical costs of the engine program. Besides, Chrysler already had one of the most

The 1966 Plymouth Belvedere I HP2, one of the first cars in which Plymouth mounted the new street Hemi engine. Never before had a manufacturer offered such a potent package for use on public roads.

powerful regular production street engines available during 1964 in its 365-horsepower, 426-cubic-inch RB.

Yet people still mythologized the mighty 390-horsepower Hemi from the previous decade. The Hemi had developed its own mystique, and the marketing folks at Chrysler wanted to capitalize on the halo effect a new Hemi would have across Chrysler's entire product line.

On February 6, 1965, styling manager J.C. Guenther and H.R. Steding, who was in charge of engine development, each received a memo jointly written by Robert Cahill and Bob Rodger. This document, perhaps the most famous memo in the history of the U.S. auto industry, had the rather dry title: "Hemi Performance Option Super Stock and 'A' Stock Competition." It outlined the following directive:

Please release a hemispherical combustion chamber engine for "B" Series [referring to the companies midsize B-body cars, which were in the process of being redesigned for the 1966 model year] with the following general characteristics:

1. Intake manifold to have two four-barrel carburetors.
2. Cylinder block to maintain cross tie bolt main bearing caps.
3. Cast Iron exhaust manifold.
4. Solid lifters are acceptable but not preferred.
5. Pistons—forged are acceptable and thermally controlled preferred.
6. Manifolding and camshaft to be designed to give the best high-speed power possible while still maintaining a reasonably drivable vehicle for summer and winter.
7. Automatic and four-speed transmissions required (four-speed to have development priority).
8. No air conditioning required for "B" Series.
9. Limited warranty is acceptable for "B" Series usage . . .

This engine to replace eight-barrel wedge requested in Product Planning Letter . . . dated 8/5/64.

Page 194- 195: In 1967 Dodge introduced the Coronet R/T (Road and Track) as a companion to the Charger muscle car. Basically a Charger with more conservative styling, the Coronet R/T offered an optional Hemi engine. This is a 1969 model.

Page 196-197: (Main) Dodge redesigned the Coronet for 1968, but only a year later the new look's clean lines were somewhat muddied up by a pastiche of tacked on ornamentation like fake hood and side scoops. But with a Hemi under the hood, the car had the go to back up the show. *(Inset)* A pair of four-barrel carburetors fed the 425 horsepower street Hemi engine, which was available as a very expensive option in the R/T.

In the early part of 1966 Plymouth didn't badge the Belvedere I as a Hemi; instead, the cars were wore "HP2" fender callouts. "HP2" stood for "Horse Power Squared." As clever as this was, dealers weren't impressed—no one knew what HP2 meant. Meanwhile everyone knew what "Hemi" meant, and dealer pressure forced Plymouth to drop the "HP2" badges and replace them with "Hemi" callouts in the middle of the model year.

The hardtops might have looked cooler than the stodgy post models, but smart racers knew the posts were lighter and had more structural rigidity. A person who ordered a Belvedere I two-door post with the HP2 engine intended to do some serious racing.

This memo became one of the most published memos ever because it announced the birth of the street Hemi. According to the memo, Chrysler expected to build 5,000 to 7,500 Hemi-equipped cars per year. In reality, Chrysler sold fewer than half of the lowest production estimate for Hemi-powered B-bodies in 1966, which Rodger and Cahill probably expected all along. The inflated estimates were likely the result of the need to pad sales projections in order to create a profit-and-loss estimate that would

fly with Chrysler's board of directors. (Most P&L assessments don't include a field for "Halo Effect.")

The birth memo put the street Hemi, given the internal code A102, on a fast-track development program, thus ensuring that it hit the streets by year's end, so Chrysler's cars could qualify for the 1966 NASCAR season. The resulting street Hemi varied less from its racing sibling than one would expect, given the expense of building the race version, but

"HEMI HEAD 426." After two seasons of total domination on U.S. drag strips, that was pretty much all anyone needed to know about what was under the hoods of the newest street racers from Dodge and Plymouth.

that was in part the result of the accelerated development schedule. It would take four more years for Chrysler's engineers to develop a marginally civilized street Hemi.

Compression ratio in the street engine dropped to a more reasonable 10.25:1, allowing the engine to run on the highest grade pump gas then available. If an owner needed to refill the tank on a car equipped with a race Hemi, he (and political correctness aside, virtually all race Hemis were owned by he's instead of she's) needed to make a trip to the local airport or the nearest racetrack to get the fuel with the octane rating required by the car's 12.5:1 compression pistons.

In an attempt to make the Hemi more streetable, engineers used a camshaft with less lift and overlap. They lowered valve spring rates to make the valvetrain more reliable at steady rpm, and also to lower the rev limit to bring power output down to the advertised 425 horsepower. They swapped the cross-ram intake manifold with an aluminum unit that mounted the two Carter four-barrel carburetors in a parallel line above the engine's camshaft. Instead of the chrome valve covers used on the race engine, the street Hemi featured valve covers coated in a black crinkle finish.

In a cost-saving move that would address one of the few weak links in the early race Hemis, Chrysler engineers replaced the tubular steel headers of the race engine with cast-iron exhaust manifolds.

Other than these changes, the new street Hemi was pretty much identical to the race version. It used the same double-roller timing chain, the same rugged rocker-arm system, and the same optional heavy-duty A727B Torqueflite automatic transmission. Chrysler built the street Hemis to near-race specifications because they knew that a good number of the cars—perhaps the majority—would end up seeing the noisy side of a drag strip. Since part of the reason for the car's existence was to provide a halo effect for the entire Chrysler lineup, the company needed the street Hemi to withstand the rigors of drag racing. Cars that broke in front of huge crowds of people on Sunday weren't likely to sell in huge numbers on Monday.

Chrysler's Marine and Industrial division in Marysville, Michigan, assembled the street Hemis, giving each engine almost the same amount of individual care and testing as Tom Hoover's team had given to the race engines built at Chrysler's Highland Park lab. Even though the engines were rated at 425 horsepower, which was a pretty accurate figure for the detuned street Hemi, most buyers knew they were getting hand-built race engines that were just a few modifications away from being 500-plus horsepower drag racers.

BIRTH OF THE STREET HEMI

On January 29, 1966, Chrysler announced that it would be making street versions of the Hemi available as optional engines for the company's 1966 B-body cars: the Plymouth Belvedere and Dodge Coronet. These were crisply styled cars that have aged well and are still extremely handsome today, but in 1966 they seemed a little conservative when compared to the muscle cars being built by General Motors and Ford Motor.

But Chrysler also offered a new B-body model for 1966 that was aimed squarely at the emerging muscle car market: the upscale Dodge Charger. While the other B-body cars featured styling that wouldn't scare anyone's grandmother, the Charger had the sleek, sexy look a car needed to go up against the likes of the GTO and Malibu SS, thanks to its sculpted fastback roofline. The Charger had other styling touches that set it apart from the crowd, including headlights hidden behind doors in the grill and bucket seats not only in the front, but in the back as well. Budget constraints kept much of the Coronet's sheet metal on the Charger, but

In 1966 Dodge introduced an all-new muscle car to go along with its new street Hemi engine: the Charger. To create the Charger, Dodge added a fastback roofline to the basic B-body hardtop coupe.

Like the C-300 before it, the new Charger was a luxurious performance car rather than a barebones street-fighter, and buyers could order just about any option Dodge offered for the car. Fortunately, the option list included the Hemi engine.

no one would confuse the two. Visually, the Charger had enough unique content to distinguish it from Grandma's grocery-getter.

The Charger proved an ideal home for the street Hemi. If a buyer was rich enough and brave enough to spend the extra $1,105 needed to check the "Hemi" box on the option sheet, he or she had one of the fastest muscle cars built at the time. Even though it was heavy, at 4,390 pounds, a 1966 Charger with a street Hemi was good for a 14.16 second quarter-mile. From there, an owner could improve that number dramatically by opening up the exhaust and mounting a set of sticky tires—the Hemi could spin the original-equipment Blue Streak street rubber down to the cords in short order.

Chrysler marketed the new Charger to the emerging Baby Boom market, a massive group of consumers who were driving the U.S. auto market in 1966. Ad copy for the new Hemi-powered Charger attempted to capture the youth lexicon of the period (with limited success), making obvious references to Ford's popular Mustang:

> Dodge Charger with a big, tough 426 Hemi up front makes other steeds look staid. Both for show and go. Charger looks beautiful standing still. And the optional Hemi V-8 supplies a kick to match, with 425 muscular horses. Not a pony or a kitten in the bunch. The hot setup? You bet.

Plymouth also introduced a more upscale B-body model for 1966: the Belvedere Satellite. Unlike the Charger, which had unique fastback bodywork, the Satellite was basically a Belvedere with a tasteful chrome trim package.

Fitting the massive 426 Hemi in the engine bay of Chrysler's B-body cars took more than a little ingenuity. The right front shock tower had to be modified to make room for the engine, and the booster cylinder for the brakes had to be moved. Even so, the cylinder had to be removed to adjust the valves, an all-too frequent occurrence. The brake cylinder had to be removed just to get access to the rear-most spark plug on the driver's side. No one ever accused a street Hemi of being user friendly.

The automotive press made a complete spectacle of its collective self trying to find superlatives superlative enough to describe Chrysler's amazing new engine. In the October 1965 issue of *Hi-Performance Cars*, Martyn Schorr wrote: "This engine is without a doubt the hottest hunk of iron to hit the street in the last ten years." The following March, Schorr described driving 160 miles per hour in a Plymouth street Hemi in the pages of the magazine:

> We made the trek in record time, occasionally opening up all eight barrels to prevent the high torque hemi from feeling neglected! The transition from two to four and then to eight barrels was smooth as silk and the hemi really didn't feel its oats until the tach needle soared past the 3,800 rpm mark. And we really mean soared!

LOWERED EXPECTATIONS

The Charger proved a hit with buyers, and Chrysler sold 37,334 of them in 1966, though only 468 buyers—1.2 percent of all Charger customers that year—elected to equip their cars with the expensive Hemi engine.

The other 98.8 percent drove off with the 325-horsepower 383-cubic-inch B-block. Occupying the next step down on the Chrysler engine hierarchy in 1966, the B-block made much more sense for the average driver. In his book *Muscle Car Confidential: Confessions of a Muscle*

The 727 TorqueFlight automatic transmission was a good choice for transmitting the Hemi's prodigious torque to the rear wheels, and the automatic cars were actually quicker in the quarter mile than the four-speed cars.

The Charger's fastback styling was striking when it first appeared, but it didn't age well and soon appeared somewhat Baroque next to the clean, classical lines of the muscle cars coming from GM and Ford. Sales were strong in 1966 but fell off precipitously in 1967.

Car Test Driver (Motorbooks, 2007), author Joe Oldham describes his attitude toward the Hemi at the time: "The Hemi engine was better suited to full-throttle operation on a racetrack (after a blueprinting and supertuning) than to street use. The huge sewer-size ports and twin 4-barrel carbs made zero low-end torque and the solid lifters had to be adjusted every two miles." In addition to saving the buyer $1,000 when compared to the Hemi, the 383 Charger was as quick from 0-to-60 as the expensive Hemi, thanks to its 425 lb-ft of torque, which edged out the 420 lb-ft of torque produced by the Hemi. Of course, by the quarter-mile point, the Hemi disappeared into the distance, leaving the 383 for dead, but in that era most performance contests in the United States took place over a distance of one-quarter mile or less.

Likewise, buyers of the other B-body cars chose the Hemi in more limited quantities than predicted. Plymouth's new Belvedere Satellite sold well, with the division moving 38,158 examples, but just 530 of those had Hemi engines. In all, instead of the projected 5,000–7,500 units, Chrysler sold 2,428 Hemi-equipped B-bodies for the 1966 model year.

For most people the Hemi was simply too much engine. Even those people who could afford the steep asking price seldom had the skill to handle a car with that powerful an engine. Regardless of whether or not they could drive the car, the few people who did check the Hemi box on the option sheet certainly got their money's worth in bragging rights; any discussion about who had the fastest car in town usually ended the instant someone said, "I've got a Hemi. . . ." The street Hemi might not have been the most popular choice for Charger power, but its very existence escalated the muscle car performance wars raging in Detroit.

Closer examination reveals that the fastback styling wasn't really integrated into the B-body lines as much as it was set on top of the existing car.

Quite a few of the Hemi cars did find homes with serious racers. Since Chrysler focused its resources on developing the street Hemi, the company didn't offer a Super Stock or drag racing special for 1966. Instead, racers had to buy production cars and convert them to race-spec themselves. Since the strongest and lightest available body style was the unlovely two-door post sedan, which had much less pleasing lines than the stylish (but less rigid and heavier) hardtops, it's a fair bet that many of the Hemi-powered two-door post cars sold in 1966 ended up competing at drag strips around the country. That equates to 83 Dodge Coronets and 136 Plymouth Belvederes.

To appeal to drag racers, Chrysler offered a series of optional deletes that both saved weight and reduced the purchase price. For example, if a buyer was savvy enough to order option code 416, he could have the heater and radio deleted, saving weight and $70.32 in the process. After that, a buyer could rely on the burgeoning aftermarket to convert his car into a full-on drag racer.

RETURN TO DAYTONA

When Chrysler made the Hemi a regular production option that was available in its passenger cars, NASCAR had no choice but to allow the Hemi back on its superspeedways. In 1966 Richard Petty started the Daytona 500 from pole position and drove his Petty Enterprises-prepared Plymouth Satellite to victory. Petty led the race for 108 laps, and Paul Goldsmith, another Plymouth driver, led for another 43 laps before falling to the back of the pack because of mechanical difficulties.

In all, Hemi-powered Chryslers accounted for seven of the top-10 spots in that year's race. David Pearson, who finished third in a Cotton Owens-prepared Dodge Charger, went on to win 15 races that season, earning Dodge a Grand National championship. This was the most victories one driver had earned in a single season since Tim Flock had won 18 races in one of Carl Kiekhaefer's C-300s in 1955. In all, Hemi-powered cars earned 34 victories in the 1966 Grand National series.

Chrysler dominance became even more complete in 1967. The Hemis got off to a rough start, getting beaten badly by the Holman-Moody prepared Fords driven by Mario Andretti and Fred Lorenzen at Daytona, but Petty went on to earn 27 Grand National wins, a record that stands to this day, and he easily clinched the 1967 Grand National championship.

MARKETING MUSCLE

The 1966 B-body cars sold well enough for Chrysler, though the model designed for the youth market—the Charger—failed to strike a chord with baby boomers. Compared to the 72,272 Chevelle SS 396s Chevrolet sold, the 96,946 GTOs Pontiac sold, and the breathtaking 607,568 Mustangs Ford sold, the 37,344 Chargers that Dodge sold indicated that the division's interpretation of a sporty car wasn't connecting with baby boomers.

For 1967, Chrysler offered a pair of new B-body models aimed squarely at the muscle car market: The Dodge Coronet R/T, which stood for "Road and Track," and the Plymouth GTX,

The GTX was the only Plymouth that was supposed to receive the Hemi engine for 1967, but a few of the mighty power plants found their ways into more pedestrian Belvederes.

which apparently stood for nothing in particular but sounded like a car that could kick a GTO's ass. These cars still featured the rather conservative bodywork of the 1966 models, but with their nonfunctional hood scoops (the R/T featured one centrally mounted scoop, a miniature faux version of the scoop from the Super Stock cars, and the GTX had a pair of fake scoops above either cylinder bank) they were a step in the right direction, something to attract buyers while Chrysler prepared radically restyled cars for the 1968 model year.

Each car could be ordered with an optional Hemi, which was little changed from the 1966 engine. The base engine in both cars was a new high-performance wedge design that offered better street performance than the Hemi. In 1966 Chrysler had introduced a 350-horsepower 440-cubic-inch RB engine for its full-sized luxury cars, the Imperial and New Yorker. When mounted in the sporty 1967 B-body muscle cars, the engine received a hot rodding treatment consisting of special heads with 10 percent larger valves and stiffer valve springs, hotter camshafts, and a huge Carter

In 1967 no fender callout spoke louder than those proclaiming: "426 Hemi."

Though the design has aged well—its clean, crisp lines look especially handsome today—in 1967 the squared-off Belvedere-based GTX looked decidedly frumpy and old-fashioned.

AFB four-barrel carburetor. These tricks raised the horsepower rating to 375, the highest of any engine equipped with hydraulic lifters at the time.

But peak horsepower was not what this engine was all about. It was about torque, lots and lots of tire-smoking torque. The engine, labeled "440 Magnum" when mounted in a Dodge and the "440 Super Commando" when mounted in a Plymouth, churned out a class-leading 480 lb-ft of torque. This meant that the base-model GTX or R/T would outrun the same car

Chrysler's designers gave the GTX a sporty interior with all the accoutrements that a muscle-car buyer expected in 1967, such as bucket seats and a floor-shifted transmission.

The GTX came with a high-performance version of the 440-cubic-inch RB engine as standard equipment; the only optional engine was the Hemi.

equipped with an optional (and expensive) Hemi in an impromptu stoplight drag, at least in stock form. Thus, not a lot of people went into debt to order a Hemi for cars that were going to live their lives on the street instead of on the track.

The year 1967 was not a good one for restraint, and Chrysler's B-bodies, with their restrained styling, suffered mightily. Charger sales fell to just 14,980 units, and sales of all three B-bodied muscle cars—the Charger, Coronet R/T, and GTX—totaled a mere 37,176 units, less than the Charger had sold alone the previous year. Hemi sales declined precipitously; only 1,121 buyers found the testicular fortitude to equip their B-body cars with the expensive Hemi engine in 1967, less than half the number sold in 1966. Apparently the new 440 was taking a hefty bite out of the Hemi's diminishing piece of the market pie.

DRAG PACKAGE

While Chrysler dealers lamented the downturn in sales, Mopar drag racing enthusiasts had something to cheer about in 1967: a special run of Hemi cars equipped with a drag racing package. These were cars designed to compete in the NHRA's Super Stock/B class. In what seemed a contradictory move, Chrysler built these modified Belvederes (production code RO23) and Coronets (production code WO23) using two-door hardtop bodies rather than the lighter, stronger two-door post sedans. This was because hardtops were more popular than posts. Chrysler's primary motivation for building such cars was to drive traffic to Dodge and Plymouth showroom floors, so the race department decided that the competition cars should look like the street cars people actually wanted to buy.

Each of these cars was identically prepared, with white paint and black vinyl interiors. The cars retained stock bodywork and didn't use any lightweight fiberglass or aluminum panels. The only outward clue to the true nature of the drag package cars was the steel hood scoop needed to feed air into the gaping maw of the Carter carburetors.

Automatic-equipped cars came with an 8.75-inch Chrysler differential that housed 4.86:1 gears, and the four-speed cars came with a Dana 60 that housed 4.88:1 gears. The A-833 four-speed transmissions were modified to what Chrysler called "Slick-Shift" specification, where the synchronizers were removed and every other tooth was machined off the engagement gears. This system really was slick for full-on clutchless power shifting, but it was lousy for street use. The engine was a standard A102 street Hemi with a modified intake manifold that used a pair of modified Carter carburetors.

The Dodge listed for $3,875 and the Plymouth listed for $3,831. Since no options were available (though a few buyers managed to add a small gee-gaw or three to the order sheet), these cars were identical to one another except for a slight crease here or there in the bodywork, so it's hard to see Chrysler's logic in pricing the Dodge $44 higher than the Plymouth. As had been the case in 1964 and 1965, the price of these drag specials didn't include a warranty, real or implied, and each car carried the now-familiar warning: "This model is intended for use in supervised acceleration trials and is not intended for highway or general passenger car use."

Chrysler restyled its B-body cars for 1968, giving them cleaner, more modern lines. Plymouth's top-of-the-line muscle car for that year was the Hemi GTX convertible.

ROAD RUNNERS AND SUPER BEES

Up until this point, Chrysler had relied on its engineering prowess to compensate for its shortcomings in styling. As had been the case with the early pre-Virgil Exner Hemis, the public turned away from Chrysler's dated designs. This was a difficult fall from grace for a company that had become famous for the stylish cars that flowed from Virgil Exner's pen.

Chrysler spent much of the 1960s trying to catch up with the competition when it came to auto styling. When the Charger hit the streets in 1966, it found itself a couple of years behind the competition. Had the competition been the 1964 A-bodies from General Motors—the GTO,

The convertible body style was never a popular platform in which to mount Hemi engines. The powerful mills required more structural rigidity to transmit their torque into forward motion than a convertible could offer.

As with the previous generation of B-body muscle cars, the redesigned Charger, with its hidden headlights, was the most distinctive of the redesigned B-body cars. Shown is a 1970 example.

The standard engine in the Charger R/T was the high-performance version of the 440-cubic-inch RB engine. The only engine Dodge offered as an option was the 426 Hemi.

The Charger's racing-style fuel-filler cap hinted at the car's NASCAR racing heritage, but its tunnel-like rear window, stylish as it was, was aerodynamically awful, and hampered Dodge's efforts on NASCAR superspeedways.

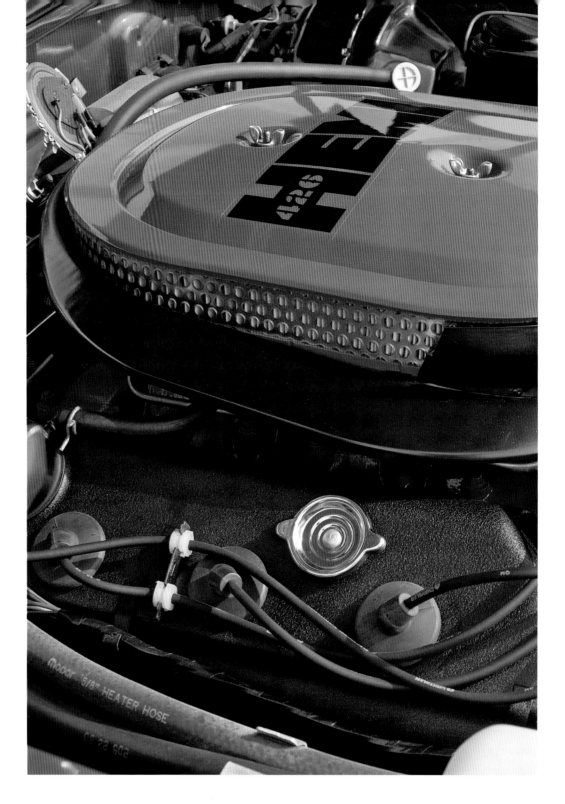

Chevelle, Skylark, and F-85 Cutlass—the Charger might have appeared more contemporary. Instead, Chrysler dropped the Charger into a market where it would have to compete with restyled A-bodies from General Motors. Instead of the slab-sided body panels of the original A-cars, the 1966 models featured what was referred to as "Coke-bottle" styling. Cars earned this nickname by having more rounded body panels with arcs over the wheel wells, making them resemble bottles of Coca-Cola laid on their sides.

For 1968, Chrysler applied its interpretation of the Coke-bottle styling treatment to its struggling B-body cars. The resulting machines, with their smooth lines, subtly rounded curves, and near-perfect proportions, were some of the most stunning automobiles of the classic muscle car era.

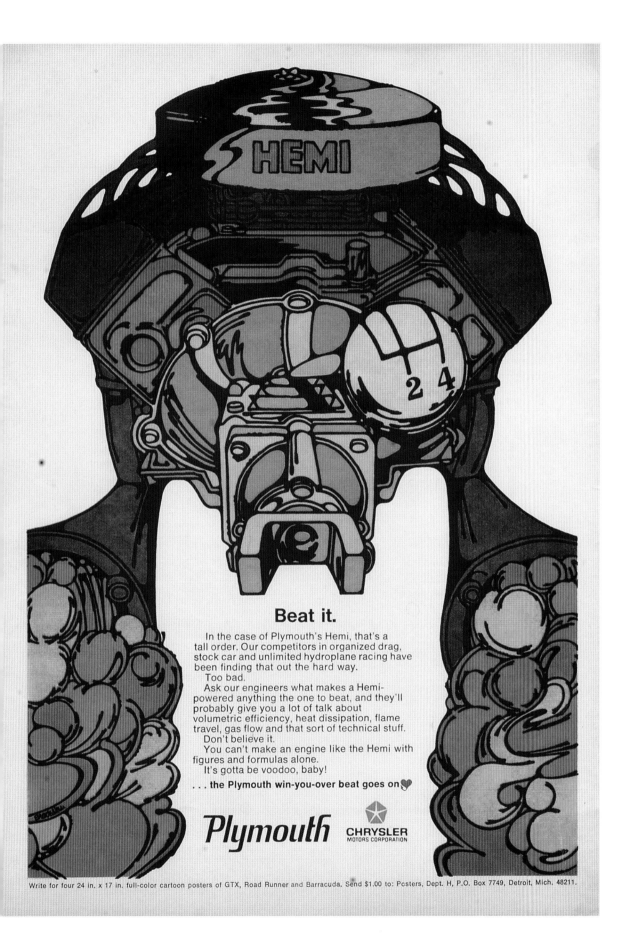

Dodge introduced a restyled Charger and Coronet R/T for 1968, along with a new R/T rendition of the Charger. The Charger took the Coke bottle shape farther than any of the other B-body cars. The R/T version differed from the standard Charger primarily in the addition of a few cosmetic badges, though it did include one critically important piece of standard equipment: the 375-horsepower 440. Of course the Hemi was an option. When Tom McCahill tested a Hemi-powered 1968 Charger R/T for the December 1967 issue of *Mechanix Illustrated*, he described the car as being "as wild as a Killarney bat after a quick dip into a tub of LSD."

Chrysler made some improvements to the street Hemi for 1968. A slightly higher compression ratio (10.3:1) and a revised camshaft (still with solid lifters) bumped torque to 490 lb-ft (though horsepower remained at 425), putting the Hemi back on top of

In 1968 Plymouth licensed a popular Warner Brothers cartoon character for the name of its budget-priced muscle car: the Road Runner.

Chrysler's performance ladder. Buyers once again had a reason to dig deep into their wallets to get the Hemi option.

Plymouth added a companion model for the GTX, a raw street racer even more barebones than the R/T. This represented a move in the opposite direction from the trends that muscle cars had been following throughout the decade. They had grown larger, heavier, more luxurious—in other words, flabbier. Plymouth thought there might be a market for a trimmed-down hot rod. They stripped the restyled B-body chassis of all frills like bucket seats and carpeting, endowed the car with the heavy-duty suspension from Chrysler's police package, and gave it the 335-horsepower version of the 383 as the base engine. Best of all, they priced the car at $2,896, making it the performance bargain of the classic muscle car era.

The standard engine in the 1968 Road Runner and Super Bee was a version of the 383-cubic-inch, B-block wedge V-8 with freer-flowing heads. But a buyer could upgrade to potent Hemi power if he (or she) was willing to spend the money.

After seeing how successful Plymouth's barebones Road Runner had been, Dodge introduced its own cartoon muscle car, the Super Bee, later in the 1968 model year. This is a 1969 model.

As in the Road Runner, the only optional engine available for the Super Bee in 1968 was the Hemi. For 1969 a buyer could select an optional 440-cubic-inch RB engine with three two-barrel carburetors.

Restraint hadn't been working so well for Chrysler; with the Road Runner, restraint went the way of the push-button transmission. In one of the most outrageous marketing moves of the period, Plymouth licensed the use of a popular Warner Brothers' cartoon character and named the car Road Runner. The hot rod Plymouth featured graphics of the cartoon bird as well as a dual-toned horn designed to ape the Road Runner's distinctive "meep-meep" voice. This was not a machine for a shrinking violet who wanted an inconspicuous car.

Best of all, the Road Runner could be ordered with the improved 426 Hemi. When equipped with a Hemi, the lightweight Road Runner became the fastest regular production street car of the 1960s.

Rather than licensing a cartoon character as Plymouth had done, Dodge elected to invent its own cartoon character, the Super Bee, which was a pun on the car's B-body origins.

Encouraged by the success of the Road Runner, Dodge developed its own cartoon car midway through the 1968 sales year. Rather than license an existing cartoon character, Dodge created its own: the Super Bee. Like the Road Runner, the Super Bee was a stripped-down version of Dodge's B-body coupe—the Coronet—that came with a standard 383 Magnum engine and a four-speed transmission. And like the Road Runner, the Super Bee could be ordered with an optional 426 Hemi engine.

HEMI A-BODIES

Most people looking to race a Mopar product in 1968 bought one of the stripped-down B-body cars—the Road Runner or the Super Bee—and ordered the optional Hemi engine. From there, they built their own drag cars using aftermarket parts and/or parts from Chrysler's Mopar parts division. As was the case in 1966, Chrysler offered no turnkey racing version of the B-body in 1968.

Early in 1968 Chrysler announced that it was going to build a special run of A-body cars—the Plymouth Barracuda and the Dodge Dart Super Stock—with Hemi engines.

Shown here is a 1968 Dart, of which only 80 were built.

The lift-off hood was made of lightweight fiberglass, as were the fenders. The metal body shell was acid-dipped to make the Dart Super Stock as light as possible.

The Hemi engine in the Dart Super Stock was basically stock. But given how incredibly light the car was—it weighed in at around 3,000 pounds— the end result was a package that was virtually unbeatable in a wide variety of drag racing classes.

The Hemi-powered B-bodies performed well, but some hard-core racers wanted more. And the factory race development folks had plenty more in the works. Late in 1967 Dick Maxwell, who worked for Bob Cahill in product planning for race development, proposed building the racing department's most radical racing concept yet. On February 20, 1968, they sent a letter to dealers explaining what that concept would be: Hemi engines stuffed in the company's small A-body cars, the Plymouth Barracuda (sales code B029) and the Dodge Dart Super Stock (sales code L023). The engine was basically a bone-stock street Hemi, but when mounted in one of these extremely light cars (3,000 pounds), the result was one of the most potent racing specials built during the classic muscle car era.

These cars were designed to fall within the rules of all major sanctioning organizations— they would not have, for example, rear axles that were moved forward 15 inches in the chassis. To comply with NHRA regulations, they were given a production code (code 366) and received VIN numbers, meaning they could conceivably be licensed for street use. In order to meet NHRA homologation requirements, which had recently been lowered, Chrysler built 70 Hemi Barracudas and 80 Hemi Darts.

These cars started out life on the assembly line at Chrysler's Hamtramck, Michigan plant, complete with 383-cubic-inch B-block engines but without any carpet or sound insulation, and

The Dart Super Stock was a pure race car, as its standard-equipment roll cage will attest. But each of these rare machines received production codes and VIN registration numbers, so they could conceivably have been registered as street cars.

were shipped to Hurst Performance, where they received their Hemi engines. The cars were then shipped back to a storage facility in Detroit, where most buyers came and picked them up.

The cars they received were body-in-white units still waiting to be painted in the owner's racing livery. The front fenders and hood were made of fiberglass and finished in black gel coat, rather than the gray primer that covered the metal body panels. In order to save weight, there were no hinges on the hood; the entire assembly was held in place by four pins and lifted straight up. (Late in the following year, this design would see use on the A12 B-body cars.) The doors and front bumper were acid dipped to further reduce weight.

Testing showed these cars to be capable of breaking into the 10-second quarter-mile bracket, and with a little tweaking could easily dip down into the 9s. Since they were basically stock production cars, they qualified for a wide variety of different classes, making them very desirable race cars. Chrysler sold every one it built before the last car left Hurst's shop.

FLEXING MOPAR MUSCLE

Sales of the redesigned 1968 Charger exploded to nearly 100,000 units, topping the sales of Pontiac's GTO, which *Motor Trend* magazine had named its car of the year. Nearly 75,000 Charger buyers chose the standard 383-equipped car, and the bulk of the rest selected the 440-equipped R/T. The remaining hard-core types bought the brutal Hemi.

Chrysler's other B-bodied muscle cars sold well, too, especially the barebones Road Runner. Plymouth moved 44,595 examples of their outrageous cartoon cars for 1968. The Super Bee also sold well, pushing total sales of B-body muscle cars to 173,872 units. This was on top of the sales of pedestrian B-body Coronets, Belvederes, and Satellites, which totaled 582,315 units. The year 1968 was a very good one for Chrysler Corporation.

Perhaps the most remarkable statistic for all of 1968, at least regarding automobile sales, was the doubling of the number of buyers selecting Chrysler's optional Hemi engine. Chrysler sold 2,276 Hemi-powered B-bodies in 1968. Almost half of those elephant engines ended up in the lightweight Road Runner. This may have been due to the fact that the Hemi was the only optional engine for Road Runner buyers wanting to step up from the 383 B-block engine—a 440-cubic-inch RB engine wouldn't become available in the Road Runner until late in the following year.

NASCAR TROUBLE

By 1968, the development of normally aspirated push-rod V-8 engines had reached the upper limits of horsepower, at least until the advent of improved electronic engine management technology. This was especially true in NASCAR racing, which had strict rules prohibiting forced induction, multiple carburetion, and fuel injection. Manufacturers wanting to win NASCAR championships had to resort to methods other than increasing raw horsepower to attain a top-speed advantage over the competition.

The most promising way to attain extra speed was to improve aerodynamic design. A small increase in aerodynamic efficiency increased top speed as much as a large increase in total horsepower output.

For 1968, Ford introduced a new car that would become the basis for its NASCAR racing effort: the Torino GT. The Torino had an aerodynamic shape that flat-out worked on NASCAR's superspeedways. Driver David Pearson dominated the 1968 season in a Holman-Moody-prepared Torino GT, winning 16 races and finishing in the top five 36 times. The Torino's aerodynamic design had helped Ford break the Hemi's recent dominance of NASCAR's Grand National series.

After getting their corporate butt handed to them in 1968, Chrysler's designers took the aerodynamically awful Dodge Charger into the wind tunnel and began crafting a car as slippery as the Ford Torino and Mercury Cyclone twins. The most notable features of the car that resulted from this work, the Charger 500, were a flush-mounted front grille and a flush-mounted rear window in place of the tunnel-type rear window used on the regular production

To combat Ford's aerodynamically efficient cars, Dodge developed the 1969 Charger 500. The recessed grille of the standard Charger was moved out flush with the front end, addressing one of the problem areas with the road car's aerodynamics.

To address the other major flaw in the Charger's aerodynamic package, Dodge's race department filled in the tunnel area of the Charger 500's back window with flush-mount glass.

The trailing edge of the Charger 500 ended with a slight lip, a token attempt at generating downforce. This wasn't enough, and Ford continued to whoop Dodge in NASCAR racing. The car Dodge would introduce for the 1970 season would change the status quo in dramatic fashion.

Charger. Though stylish, this tunnel contributed to terrible airflow over the car and held down top speeds on NASCAR track.

With the Charger 500, Chrysler took a much-improved aerodynamic package to Daytona for the running of the 1969 Daytona 500. Unfortunately for Chrysler, Ford presented an even more aerodynamic version of the Torino and Cyclone couplet, the Torino Talladega and the Cyclone Spoiler. The Ford cars used the same basic aerodynamic tricks as the Charger 500—flush grille, flush-mounted glass—to greater effect. A Ford Talladega driven by Lee Roy Yarbrough won the 500 that year and Pearson went on to win his second straight Grand National championship.

At this point Chrysler declared all-out war on Ford, as well as any other company impudent enough to challenge Mopar supremacy on NASCAR's superspeedways. Its designers went back to the wind tunnel and emerged with the single most insane automobile of the entire muscle car era: the Dodge Daytona. At its front the new Daytona featured an 18-inch prosthetic nose, designed to reduce frontal area and provide downforce at speed. In back, to balance the downforce up front, the car featured a huge wing placed on 23-inch-tall uprights. To provide downforce in racing, the wing only needed to be raised 12 inches from the rear deck, but Dodge designers placed it almost twice that high to allow the trunk lid to open on the street-going versions of the car the company would have to build to homologate the design. This aerodynamic package made the racing version of the car good for top speeds of nearly 250 miles per hour.

continued on page 238

The world had never seen a production car as dramatic as the 1970 Daytona Charger before; it will likely never see such a dramatic car again. Designed for the sole purpose of dominating NASCAR superspeedways, Dodge produced a handful of road versions in order to satisfy NASCAR's homologation regulations.

For years, Dodge's Hemi power had been enough to win on NASCAR tracks. But by 1970 brute force alone wasn't enough; the Daytona Charger was all about aerodynamic efficiency.

The reverse hood scoops on the Daytona Charger's fenders were non-functional on the road car, but they were needed on the race cars to provide clearance for the big racing tires.

With its elongated snout and exaggerated rear wing, the Daytona Charger looked more like a prop from a science-fiction film than a road-going automobile.

The Daytona Charger's huge snout stuck out 18 inches ahead of where the grille on the standard Charger was located, presenting a tortured, circuitous route for cooling air to travel on its way to the radiator.

Unlike the Spartan race cars found on NASCAR oval tracks, the road-going Daytona Charger could be optioned up as heavily as any other Charger. NASCAR drivers never had it this good.

continued from page 233

Plymouth created its own version of the winged car, the Superbird, later in the year. The Plymouth used a similar wing and nose, but had to improvise a bit on the roof design. Though the stock Road Runner had a more aerodynamically efficient rear window area than the stock Charger, the Charger's tunnel design lent itself to creating a more efficient fastback by simply covering the tunnel with a window. The rear sail area of the Road Runner had to be extended to create as efficient a design. To cover up the cobbled-together bodywork around the rear window, all production Superbirds featured vinyl roof covers.

Both cars were built offsite by a company called Creative Industries, which had to hustle to build enough street-legal cars by the January 1, 1970, deadline to homologate the car for

The rear wing didn't need to be as tall as it was to provide effective down force; it did, however, need to be that tall to enable the trunk lid to open and provide access to the spare tire.

NASCAR racing for that year. The results were worth the effort. The Mopars humiliated Ford on NASCAR tracks, winning 38 of 48 Grand National races. They would have won more, had tire technology been up to the speeds produced by the amazing winged cars. Tire failure led to some of the hairiest crashes in NASCAR history. The combined threat of deadly crashes and total Chrysler domination led Bill France to institute a rules change that would keep the winged cars off of NASCAR tracks following the 1970 season. Beginning in 1971, anything NASCAR determined was a "specialty car" (in other words, any car that Bill France thought was too odd) would have to run with a 305-cubic-inch engine. In one stroke of his rules pen, France had killed off both the winged Chryslers and the aerodynamic Fords.

When Chrysler redesigned the B-body lineup for 1971, the winged cars disappeared. Since they would not be competitive in NASCAR racing, there was little point in spending the money to develop winged versions of the new cars.

Not to be outdone by its sister division, Plymouth also developed an aerodynamic version of its B-body muscle car, the Road Runner. The resulting Superbird was even more outrageous than its Dodge sibling. This example has optional dealer-installed wheel covers that don't rotate with the wheels.

Likewise Warner Brother's cartoon bird adorns the Superbird's exaggerated rear wing. The gigantic "Plymouth" lettering was probably unnecessary, since it was pretty hard to mistake a Superbird for the offerings from rivals Ford, General Motors, or the American Motor Corporation. Or any other car ever built, for that matter.

If the 18-inch proboscis wasn't outrageous enough to attract attention, Plymouth included a decal of the Road Runner cartoon character.

Many Hemi buyers opted for steel wheels with plain hubcaps. Even though these weren't as stylish as some of the mag-type wheels offered, they were lighter and stronger, and the wheels beneath a Hemi needed to be as strong as possible to handle the engine's torque.

DUAL QUADS OR THREE DEUCES?

For 1969, Chrysler chose not to mess with a good thing, leaving its lineup largely unchanged. Likewise the Hemi engine returned unchanged, at least internally. In keeping with the psychedelic zeitgeist of the time, all Hemi-powered cars featured functional hood scoops. Owners opened and closed these cable-operated scoops via push-pull buttons mounted inside the cabs. Dodge called its system "Ramcharger," and Plymouth gave its system the catchy name "Air Grabber."

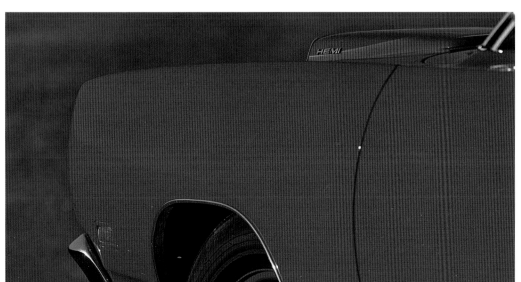

The small "Hemi" callout on the hood scoop was usually enough to scare off all but the heartiest street racers.

By 1969 the squared-off styling of the B-body muscle cars was starting to get a bit dated and sales declined from the previous year's record levels. Yet the design has aged well, and today these are considered among the most handsome cars of the classic muscle-car era.

This car led multiple lives within Chrysler Corporation. It left the assembly line as Dodge Challenger VIN number JS27R0B100022, the very first Hemi E-body convertible ever produced, and the only triple black Hemi Challenger convertible ever produced. It was rebuilt as the Yellow Jacket show car for the 1970 auto show season, then rebuilt once again as the pearl white Dodge Diamante for the 1971–75 seasons.

Halfway through the model year, the Super Bee and Road Runner models received an engine option that would provide strong competition for the Hemi: the A12. Buyers who ordered the A12 option received a trio of Holley two-barrel carburetors mounted atop a specially designed, Edelbrock-built, aluminum intake manifold feeding a high-performance 440-cubic-inch engine. In stock form this engine cranked out 390 horsepower and 490 lb-ft of torque. Because this massive reserve of twisting force was available at much lower engine speeds than was the torque of the Hemi, which had been designed to

The turn signals for the Diamante were sourced from the 1968 Barracuda. Whenever possible Chrysler used such off-the-shelf parts to keep the cost of its bespoke show cars as low as possible.

Though the source Challenger had been a convertible, the Diamante used a targa-type configuration. By 1971 convertibles appeared to be on their way towards extinction.

Also headed toward extinction was the Diamante's Hemi powerplant.

Though the targa top is a bit ungainly, the overall proportions of the Diamante are pleasing. It's a shame the design was never developed as a production car.

The Diamante's fender vents would fit right in with many of today's car designs, though it's unlikely that the car's pretty front end would pass many impact tests.

run up the top of its rev range, a well-tuned A12 car would run away from any stock Hemi at a stoplight.

To cope with the added 15 horsepower, the engine received beefier valve-train components, meaning that the A12 was built almost to the high specifications of the Hemi. Although expensive at $462.80, the A12 was still less than half of the Hemi's price.

The A12 spelled real trouble for Hemi sales. Even the guys at the Woodward Avenue garage were distracted by this new engine package. While Chrysler's NASCAR effort continued to rely on the Hemi, the stock car program was focused on aerodynamics more than engine development. The drag racing program didn't produce any Hemi-powered drag specials for 1969, choosing instead to work with the newly reinvigorated RB engine.

Hemi sales fell to 1,362 units for 1969. It seemed that the time for building hairy-chested solid-lifter race engines for the street was coming to a close.

The rear window on the Diamante is electrically powered and lowers with the flip of a switch, further enhancing the sense of open-air motoring.

MOPAR, THE NEXT GENERATION

In 1970, Chrysler continued to develop ultra-high-performance machines, even though the writing was on the wall for muscle cars. That year went down as the peak year for muscle car performance; everyone in the industry knew it would be all downhill from there. In 1971, U.S. automakers began to detune their engines with lower compression ratios, retarded ignition, milder camshafts, and increasingly restrictive intake and exhaust systems. This was in preparation for the coming of unleaded, lower-octane gasoline, which the government had mandated all cars would burn beginning with the 1975 model year.

This factory-customized 1970 Hemi Road Runner is one of the cars Plymouth built in 1970 and 1971 for its Rapid Transit System Caravan tour, which appeared at over 150 Plymouth dealers and racing events across the country.

The custom grille on the 1970 Rapid Transit System Caravan Hemi Road Runner features rectangular Cibie headlights. The Airgrabber hood scoop is fixed in the open position.

After July 1, 1974, gas stations would begin phasing out gasoline with tetraethyl lead as an additive. Lead had been added to gasoline since before World War II to prevent engine detonation, allowing the use of the higher compression ratios that enabled the Hemi to produce so much horsepower. But lead was a nasty carcinogenic substance that caused birth defects, developmental disabilities, and all sorts of problems with the environment, though its role in these problems wasn't clearly understood at the time. What was known was that the EPA planned to institute emissions requirements beginning in 1975 that would require most automakers to install catalytic converters in their exhaust system. These converters used

The large Road Runner decals on the doors were actually available for any Road Runner—only on this car the dust trails were extended by hand painting them to the quarter scoops.

platinum-coated beads to reduce the toxic emissions in automotive exhaust. Lead stuck to these beads and plugged up the exhaust system.

Not only did this curtail the future production of Hemi-powered muscle cars; it spelled trouble for the examples Chrysler had already built. By 1978 it would be virtually impossible to buy pump gas with a high-enough octane rating to prevent a high-compression Hemi engine from chewing itself to bits.

If impending government-mandated strangulation wasn't bad enough, insurance companies were starting to exert a negative influence on muscle car sales. The equation of high-horsepower,

A set of custom Ansen Sprint slotted mags filled the extra wide rear-wheel openings, and the back of the car featured a large rear spoiler, side marker lamps, and full-width taillamp treatment.

low-weight cars, plus young male drivers yielded the sum of exorbitantly high insurance premiums. While many baby boomers could afford the relatively low prices the manufacturers charged for muscle cars, they were starting to have problems affording the steep cost of insuring the beasts, and the Hemi was the most beastly muscle car of them all. If the steep purchase price of the Hemi wasn't deterrent enough for many buyers, the steep insurance costs would keep all but the most dedicated speed freak from driving a Hemi out of a Dodge or Plymouth dealership.

The future of the muscle car looked bleak, but Chrysler intended to build its powerful street fighters until the federal government pried the last Hemi from its cold, dead corporate fingers, and damn the insurance companies and the EPA.

This car was pulled off the assembly line and taken to Roman's Chariot Shop in Ohio for the body modifications, which included large rear fender flares and enlargement of the quarter-panel scoops.

Black paint stretched from the base of the windshield and rear window toward each end of the car, which, along with black stripes along the side of the car, emphasized the clean lines of the B-body.

MOPAR PONY CAR

As the 1960s came to a close, Chrysler was still not a player in the lucrative pony car market, but the company finally had plans to change that situation. To keep development costs down, Chrysler designers took the cowl and other chassis components under development for the next generation B-body cars and built a pony car around them. Internally coded the "E-bodies," the cars featured the classical proportions that Virgil Exner had admired in the sporty Italian cars of the 1940s and 1950s—long hood, short deck, small passenger compartment. These design features, which exemplified what Exner called the school of "Italian simplicity," had come to define the pony car genre.

When Chrysler finally got into the pony-car market with the Challenger and Barracuda for the 1970 model year, it made up for lost time by offering the potent Hemi as the top engine option for the cars.

The 1970 Hemi 'Cuda represents the zenith of the classic muscle-car era, offering a level of performance never before available in a street car.

While just about every other muscle car engine was slightly neutered for the 1971 model year, the Hemi kept all of its gonads intact, making the 1971 Hemi 'Cuda the unquestioned king of the quarter-mile that year.

This 1971 Hemi 'Cuda convertible is one of the most high profile examples of the breed—it served as the model for the car driven by Don Johnson in the television show *Nash Bridges*.

The E-body car was actually a pair of cars: the Dodge Challenger and Plymouth Barracuda, introduced for the 1970 model year. The Dodge Challenger rode on a wheelbase that was stretched 2 inches over its Plymouth counterpart—112 inches versus 110 inches—and overall, the Dodge pony car was 4.3 inches longer than the Plymouth. Technically, they broke little new ground, but they did blur the line between pony car and muscle car. Because they used the basic front cowl from the impending B-body redesign, the new E-bodies were larger than

their pony-car competitors from Ford or General Motors, but they were smaller than Chrysler's B-body muscle cars.

While it led to a car that was physically larger than the competition, using B-body components allowed Chrysler to offer the E-body with any engine in the company's stable, including the mighty Hemi, which, when mounted in the new E body cars, created the most potent muscle car package in the Mopar lineup.

The sporty version of the 1970 Challenger was the R/T. The R/T featured the 383-cubic-inch B-block engine with Magnum heads as its base engine, though a buyer could choose an optional 440-cubic-inch RB engine with either a single four-barrel or three two-barrel carburetors. If a buyer intended to do some serious racing, he or she ordered a 426 Hemi. The performance version of the Barracuda was simply called the 'Cuda, and had the same selection of engines.

'Cuda buyers who opted for the Hemi option received a Shaker hood scoop system as standard equipment. (Challenger buyers could order the system as an extra-cost option.) This consisted of a giant intake snorkel over the air cleaner that protruded up through a gaping hole in the hood. The system didn't lend itself to use in inclement weather and it didn't have much effect on performance one way or another, but few would argue that it is the single coolest hood scoop produced during the muscle-car era.

The year 1971 would be the end of the line for Chrysler's 426 Hemi, at least in street cars. The engine's phenomenal success on the racetrack would keep the basic design alive to this day.

The suspensions of the 1971 E-bodies were softened during the cars' sophomore year, giving them less aggressive handling, but they made up for that with a more aggressive appearance—especially the 'Cuda, which featured these shark-like gills in the front fenders.

In 1970, Chrysler installed a new hydraulic-lifter cam in the Hemi, finally eliminating periodic valve adjustments from the Hemi owner's long list of maintenance chores. Horsepower remained unchanged at 425, but given the untapped potential of the engine, it was relatively easy for Chrysler engineers to adjust horsepower up or down as needed. For anyone except a racer who intended to build a 1,000-horsepower drag motor, the hydraulic lifters were a step in the right direction. Valve adjustments were labor-intensive affairs on

The Dodge and Plymouth E-bodies weren't the most structurally rigid cars ever built, and they were even less so when their tops were chopped off. This made them unlikely platforms in which to mount Hemi engines. As a result the cars were rare and they seldom saw the business side of a racetrack. Perhaps because of this fact, the few that were built stood a better-than-average chance of surviving.

Dodge's Challenger, it's version of the E-body pony car, also offered a Hemi as its top engine option.

Although the shaker hood scoop was standard equipment on a Hemi 'Cuda, it was an extra-cost option on the Challenger.

This particular 1971 Challenger is almost certainly the most heavily optioned Hemi E-body ever built. It had every option in Dodge's catalog, including a sunroof. It even had a built-in Dictaphone, should the well-heeled Hemi-driver ever need to dictate a memo while running down the drag strip.

the big, complex Hemi, and eliminating them made the Hemi a more viable alternative for many buyers.

At least hydraulic lifters made the Hemi a more viable alternative for rich buyers; ordering a Hemi engine added $871.45 to the $3,164 base price of a 1971 'Cuda. That's dangerously close to a 30-percent price increase. In contrast, the torque-monster 440 Six-Pack added just $250 to the bottom line.

Because the E-body cars had been developed using basic components of the larger B-body cars, they were relatively large cars, and the Challenger was several inches longer than the 'Cuda.

Chrysler introduced completely redesigned B-body cars for the 1971 model year. These cars adopted the long-hood, short-deck proportions that Virgil Exner had championed two decades earlier.

THE LAST HEMI

Chrysler's last big money shot in the muscle car wars was its redesigned 1971 B-body platform. The new B-body models retained the Coke-bottle styling of the previous generation of cars, but adopted long-hood-short-deck pony-car proportions. Chrysler maintained the Charger, Super Bee, Road Runner, and GTX versions of the B-body chassis, but the Coronet R/T didn't make the cut. The killer big-block engines that had earned Mopar its legendary performance reputation all survived into 1971, including the Six-Pack version of the 440 and the omnipotent 426 Hemi.

Plymouth's Road Runner continued to trade on its cartoon namesake, and Chrysler continued to pay Warner Brothers a royalty for every Road Runner car that Plymouth sold.

For 1971 buyers of the redesigned B-body cars could order the Hemi engine as an option. The following year the Hemi would be extinct.

Chrysler continued to offer a manually operated functional hood scoop as standard in its Hemi-powered B-bodies.

Chrysler's designers lavished attention on the details of the corporation's muscle cars, and most versions featured extremely stylish exhaust tips, as on this 1971 Road Runner.

The Charger R/T remained the most opulent of all Chrysler muscle cars in 1971. While a physically large car, its graceful proportions made it seem much smaller.

Chrysler followed the lead of General Motors and reduced the compression ratio of the RB engine for 1971 but held the line with the Hemi. That engine returned unchanged in 1971, making it the last original muscle-car combatant still doing battle with its gonads intact.

While the Hemi didn't receive any mechanical changes for 1971, it did have a lower horsepower rating. That was because of a change in the way horsepower would be rated. Previously American automakers rated their engines in terms of SAE (Society of Automotive Engineers) gross horsepower, which was measured using a blueprinted test engine running on a stand without accessories, mufflers, or emissions control devices. This did not provide

The redesigned Charger featured exaggerated styling cues, such as these fake gills in the doors that made the gills in the 1971 'Cuda fender seem almost subdued by comparison.

By 1971 the Hemi had sprouted all sorts of hoses and other equipment in an attempt to meet EPA regulations, but the engine had so much untapped performance potential that it was relatively easy for Chrysler engineers to keep performance at pre-emissions levels.

The new-for-1971 B-bodies were some of the most stylish cars of the muscle-car era, and are just now beginning to be appreciated for their design, and not just their Hemi engines.

an accurate measurement of the power output of an engine installed in a street car. Gross horsepower figures were also easily manipulated by carmakers. They could be inflated to make a car appear more muscular or deflated to appease insurance companies or to qualify a car for a certain class of racing.

Beginning in 1972, U.S. carmakers would have to quote power exclusively in SAE net horsepower, which rated the power of the engine with all accessories and standard intake and exhaust systems installed. This provided a more accurate measurement of a given car's true output, but the overall numbers were lower.

The optional Endura bumpers on this 1971 Charger would soon go the way of the Hemi engine, as increasingly stringent impact absorption standards changed the way automobiles looked.

The 1971 Hemi-powered cars from Dodge and Plymouth were the last muscle cars of the classic era. While horsepower levels had been falling precipitously in the cars produced by other manufacturers, a 1971 Hemi could still do all the antisocial things that make us love muscle cars so much.

Chrysler began using the new rating system in 1971, giving both the old SAE gross figures and the new SAE net figures. While the old SAE gross rating remained the same for the Hemi (425 horsepower, 490 lb-ft of torque), the new SAE net rating was 350 horsepower at 5,000 rpm and the SAE net torque rating fell to 390 lb-ft at 5,000 rpm.

This was a time before online communities debated such subjects. It was before the Internet, before cable television even, and genuine information was hard to come by. Most hot rodders operated in a fog of misinformation and old wives' tales. People believed the power ratings printed in advertising brochures because often this was the only information available regarding power output. The average buyer didn't know SAE

This 1971 Charger R/T has only 11,000 original miles, and still has the paper covering the floor of its trunk. This was normally stripped out by the dealer when the car was prepped for sale.

It would be decades before American automakers built another production engine that needed as much fresh air as a Hemi.

gross from SAE net; he only knew that a Hemi with 425 horsepower was better than a Hemi with 350 horsepower.

In 1972, Chrysler further detuned its engines in preparation for the impending switch to low-octane unleaded fuel. The B-body cars could still be ordered with big-block engines, but these engines struggled to put out as much power as the small-block engines of a few years earlier. The 340-cubic-inch engine was the top offering in the E-body cars for 1972; the big-block engine had disappeared from their option lists.

And to no one's surprise, the Hemi had finally become extinct. To redesign this low-volume (Chrysler built just 486 Hemi engines in 1971), labor-intensive (each engine

Despite its size, the 1971 Charger R/T could still tear up a drag strip, at least when a 426 Hemi resided in the engine bay.

1971 would be the last year you could walk into a dealership and buy a car that was capable of winning drag races right out of the box—at least for a generation.

was still practically hand-assemble), gas-guzzling dinosaur to meet upcoming emissions regulations and run on the swill that would soon pass for pump gas would have been astronomically expensive.

Like all the other U.S. automakers of the time, Chrysler was expending every available resource in order to redesign its passenger car engines for the coming changes mandated by the government; there was simply no money available to nurse the Hemi into this brave, new world. Tom Hoover and the rest of the hot rodders at Chrysler made a valiant attempt to bring their beloved Hemi into the coming dark ages of performance cars, but the forces allied against them were inexorable.

This shortage of funds impacted every facet of Chrysler Corporation, including its racing program, which was radically curtailed for 1971. That year Chrysler only sponsored two race teams in NASCAR (which began running Winston Cup races in 1971). Richard Petty would go on to win a few more championships, but his last title in a Chrysler product came in 1975.

With the 1971 Hemi muscle cars, Chrysler rung down the curtain on the classic muscle car era.

That would also be Chrysler's last NASCAR championship—as of the end of the 2007 season Chrysler has not won another NASCAR championship.

Support money for drag racing also dried up. Dodges and Plymouths ruled the Pro Stock and Super Stock classes, and there was little need to waste limited resources to humiliate the competition even further. Tom Hoover and his crew continued to develop the Hemi for top racers like Ronnie Sox and Dick Landy, but there would be no more production runs of specialized drag racing cars.

Without the excuse of building Hemi cars to support racing activities, and with the sales of street Hemis so low as to be almost immeasurable, further Hemi production was unjustifiable. Almost before anyone realized what was happening, the Hemi disappeared, and one of the most exciting periods in automotive history had come to an end. ■

A NEW GENERATION

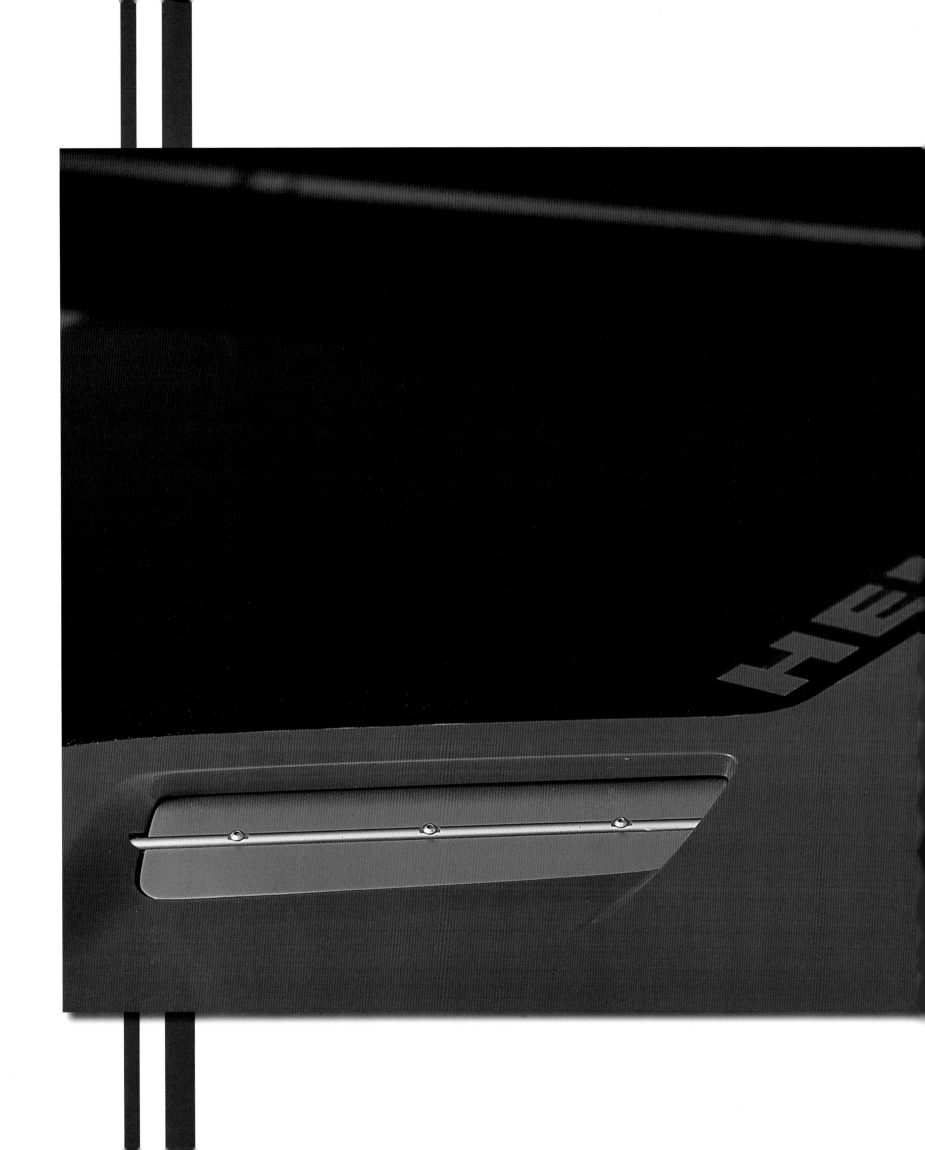

A NEW GENERATION

Even though making any sort of legitimate business case for the Hemi would have been impossible, the engineering types at Chrysler loved their big elephant engine and would make heroic efforts to keep it alive into the 1970s. They even developed the A279 Hemi, a completely new engine originally intended to be introduced for the 1972 model year.

This engine, known internally as the ball-stud Hemi, would have maintained a high level of performance while still complying with upcoming emissions standards. The new Hemi would have the added benefit of being much cheaper to produce than the 426, which appealed to Chrysler's bean counters. It would even be cheaper to produce than the wedge engines. Cost savings would come from a new, less-complicated valve operating system that used ball-studs at each stamped-metal rocker arm, much like the system used in General Motors engines, instead of the forged rocker arm and shaft system that Chrysler had always used in its high-performance engines.

If all had gone according to plan, the engine would have been built in both 400-cubic-inch and 440-cubic-inch forms. The performance of the 440 version would fall midway between the Hemi and the four-barrel version of the RB engine. Chrysler engineers got as far as testing prototype ball-stud Hemis, but in the end Chrysler decided to pass on the A279 design. The future of high-performance cars was looking grim by 1972.

THE DONOVAN 417

Even though Chrysler stopped building the street Hemi after 1971, the engine's phenomenal success at the drag strip meant there would continue to be a small specialty market that needed the engine. Ed Donovan had already begun to fulfill the demands of that market even before the original street Hemi went out of production.

Dodge tapped into a live nerve with the release of the new Ram truck in 2002 with its "big" truck look. Then they raised the ante in '03 when they dropped a new-generation Hemi in the popular pick-up.

Page 278–279: Dodge reintroduced the Challenger for 2008. The car was built to be a modern interpretation of the classic E-body design.

Page 280-281: (Main) Unlike the original Challenger, which had fake hood scoops, the *Challenger Concept* car featured functional hood scoops that opened and closed automatically. *(Inset)* The 6.1-liter Hemi engine in the 2008 Challenger SRT-8 puts out as much net horsepower (425) as the 7-liter Hemi of the 1960s put out gross. When comparing net horsepower figures, the new car beats the original by 75 horsepower.

A discrete badge on the front fender proclaims that the potent 5.7-liter Hemi is ready to haul. Ability to blur the scenery comes standard.

This isn't difficult to do, as 345 horses can overwhelm street tires with ease. The 5.7-liter Hemi was originally designed for truck duty.

In 1957 Donovan, a drag racer who cut his teeth in the aftermarket industry working at Offenhauser, started Donovan Engineering, a manufacturer of aftermarket speed equipment focusing on the needs of drag racing. Donovan was a big fan of the 392 Hemi, and his ultimate ambition was to build and market an aluminum block based on that engine, only without the early Hemi's flaws. With all the aftermarket speed equipment available for the early Hemi at the time, a racer could buy Donovan's block and build a competitive racing engine.

Donovan completed the developmental work in 1970 and began production of his aluminum Hemi engine block. To ensure that all equipment designed for the factory block would bolt right on to his block, Donovan retained all the major dimensions of the original. His only change was giving the cylinders a .125-inch overbore, so his engine displaced 417 cubic inches.

Most aluminum racing blocks at the time were solid aluminum with pressed-in steel cylinder liners. All internal passages were milled into the aluminum. Donovan used an open-cast design with chrome-moly wet-sleeve liners. This design weighed less than 200 pounds and had the added advantage of allowing easy replacement of the cylinder liners. Plus it was strong enough to handle much more power than the original factory block could handle. To further strengthen the engine, Donovan increased the size of the main bearing supports, addressing a problem that Chrysler had solved with the B-block engines.

Donovan began selling his 417 Hemi to drag racers in 1971. Top Fuel racer John Wiebe raced Donovan's aluminum Hemi for the very first time at the NHRA Supernationals in Ontario, California, setting the low time of 6.53 seconds for that year's Supernationals. Wiebe was the top qualifier and finished the event in the runner-up position. By 1972 it seemed every other dragster was running a Donovan 417 Hemi, and Donovan counted drag racing royalty like Big Daddy Garlits among his satisfied customers. Donovan Engineering grew into an engine-building empire, and the firm continues to build the 417 Hemi to this day. Donovan, who died of cancer in 1989, was posthumously inducted into the Motorsports Hall of Fame in 2003.

THE KEITH BLACK 426

Keith Black was one of the people getting beaten by Donovan and his 417 Hemis. Black became involved with the hot rod culture flourishing in his native Southern California when he was still in high school. A naturally gifted mechanic, Black began to work on the engines of the drag boats that raced in California's Salton Sea. He started out small, fixing a part here and there, but as more people became familiar with his remarkable skills, he began to get more work, and his hobby turned into a career.

Early on he worked on a few Oldsmobile or Cadillac engines, since those were the first OHV V-8 engines available. When Chrysler introduced the Hemi, he focused on that power plant, because he believed it had more potential as a race engine. In 1959 he started Keith Black Race Engines. The drag racing community took note of his successful boat racing engines, and soon he was building race motors for some of the top drivers, including Don Prudhomme.

The Rumble Bee concept truck used a number of graphic styling cues from the "classic" muscle car days. But with a supercharged Hemi cranking out more than 500-horsepower, it would outrun the older iron.

When the Donovan 417 hit the scene, Black found himself losing business because people were racing Donovan's new aluminum engine instead of the factory cast-iron 426 engines Black was building. To make matters worse, Chrysler was stopping production of the 426 Hemi.

Black had already approached Chrysler with a proposal to build an aluminum-block 426, but hadn't been able to generate any traction with that idea. When the aluminum Donovan 417 came on the scene and started beating the cast-iron Chrysler Hemis, Bob Cahill and the other folks remaining at Chrysler's racing department weren't pleased. They decided to help Black with his project, provided it didn't cost Chrysler any money; by then Chrysler's racing budget was so low as to almost be a negative number. They were able to send Black the latest engineering drawings for the Hemi so he had all the proper dimensions to work with.

It took Black a couple of years to develop the engine and find quality vendors to produce it. He introduced his aluminum version of Chrysler's 426 Hemi in 1974. His engine became the industry standard—between 1975 and 1984, cars powered by Keith Black's aluminum engine blocks held every Top Fuel record.

RETURN OF THE FACTORY HEMI

For more than 30 years after the demise of the 426 Hemi, the Hemi existed only as a low-volume race engine built by specialized aftermarket manufacturers like Donovan Engineering and Keith Black Race Engines. Meanwhile Hemi-powered cars skyrocketed in value, soaring well beyond the $100,000 mark. The mythological Hemi had earned concrete exchange value.

Chrysler engineers never let go of the idea of a Hemi; it was the Hemi, after all, that had given the company its reputation for engineering excellence. If the Hemi had become a mythic creature in the world at large, it had attained an almost god-like status within the halls of Chrysler Corporation. Generation after generation of young engineers aspired to follow in the footsteps of the legendary men behind the Hemi—folks like Tom Hoover, Ev Moeller, and Bob Cahill. They were itching to build a new Hemi, and they were about to get their shot at it, thanks to a need for a new truck engine.

By the mid-1990s, the 360-cubic-inch LA-block engine powering Dodge pickup trucks needed to be replaced. After all, the basic design of the engine dated back to the poly V-8s of the 1950s. They needed an engine that was both powerful and efficient, one that would meet upcoming emissions standards for years to come. Rich Schaum proposed building a new V-8 in 1996, and Robert Lee, who was in charge of engine development, organized a team to begin development work.

Lee's team studied every engine system on the market—overhead cams, four-valves-per cylinder heads, alternative combustion chamber designs—and discovered that the flat-six in Porsche's new Boxster was one of the most efficient engines being built. The Boxster featured domed combustion chambers. Lee and his crew looked further into the benefits of a Hemi head and the more they looked, the more benefits they found. What was a good idea in the 1940s remained a good idea in the 1990s.

Low profile tires tend to limit any vehicle's off-road ability, but the prototype Rumble Bee wasn't designed to roll onto a construction site. Granted, it was built to haul, but a different kind of cargo…

Want power, a lot of power? Just bolt on a Kenne Bell 2.2 Liter Blowzilla Supercharger and an intercooler onto your 5.7-liter Hemi, and then stand back. While more than 500 horses live in there, you can still drive to the grocery store without a complaint.

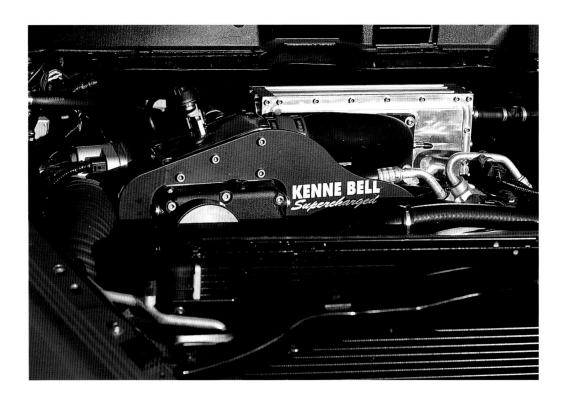

Most people are dazzled by the SpectraFlair B-5 Blue paint, but the small emblem on the fender deserves attention and respect.

Lee locked his team away in Chrysler's technical center in Auburn Hills, Michigan, to explore this concept further. They worked to develop a hemispherical combustion chamber design that was as efficient at reducing emissions as it was at producing power. The engine they came up with features an iron block with aluminum cylinder heads. The cylinders have but two valves apiece, making this a true Hemi rather than a pent-roof design like the four-valve Porsche engine. Unlike the Hemis of old, the new version is a longer-stroke design, though it is still slightly oversquare, with bore and stroke measuring 3.9-inches and 3.6-inches, respectively, for a total displacement of 5.7 liters (or 345 cubic inches, in muscle car language). In base form, it puts out 340 horsepower and 387 lb-ft of torque. The main bearing caps are held in place by two vertical bolts, along with a pair of cross bolts.

Lee's team managed to keep the new Hemi's existence a secret until it was just about to be made public. To help keep the Hemi development project from being exposed, they never referred to it as a "Hemi," even though the engine used hemispherical combustion chambers.

Although this was to ensure secrecy, part of the reason the new engine was not called a Hemi stemmed from respect for the Hemi name within Chrysler. By this time the Hemi had become acknowledged as the single greatest engineering accomplishment of any American auto manufacturer during the classic muscle car era, and you did not take the name Hemi in vain at Chrysler. If Lee and his engineers were going to use the name Hemi, the engine they produced had to be damned good. They wouldn't call it a Hemi until it had proved its worth. It did. The engine handled every durability torture test to which the team subjected it.

Looking like it would be right at home on the headrest of a 1970 Super Bee muscle car, the Rumble Bee concept truck "borrowed" the theme from the automobile to create an eye-catching, fun truck.

Yes, these exhaust tips are NOS 1970 Super Bee units. When you're building a concept vehicle, inspiration can come in many forms. And yes, they sound great.

The concept for the hot Dodge Rumble Bee Ram pickup truck was designed and built by Larry Weiner's Performance West Group. Not just a pretty face, the concept truck is a fully functioning, street-legal monster.

THAT THING GOT A HEMI?

The engine originally debuted in the 2003 model year pickups. Since the engine had proven worthy of the name Hemi, Chrysler's marketing folks made good use of that name, plastering it all over the new trucks. They even made it the central component of a wildly successful advertising campaign. This campaign consisted of a couple of losers in a rust-bucket car pulling up to the new Dodge pickup and asking the pickup driver, "That thing got a Hemi?" Of course it did, and of course the pickup driver exited the scene in a blaze of burnt rubber. When he's gone, the dill weed in the rust bucket said, "Sweet."

The ad told the world that Chrysler fully recognized the iconic status that its Hemi engine had achieved. And it made clear that the company (which was then part of DaimlerChrysler) knew how to market that icon to maximum effect.

Part of marketing the iconic Hemi engine involved mounting it in something sportier than a truck. Pickups are an important source of revenue for any U.S. automaker, but they aren't muscle cars, so for 2004 Chrysler introduced a brand new 300C. Chrysler had revived the "300" nameplate several years earlier, but the car to which the name was attached—the 300M—had been a milque-toast front-wheel-drive sedan. The completely new 300C was a fire-breathing, rear-wheel-drive, muscular machine, thanks to its Hemi engine.

Chrysler showed the new 300C concept car at the California Auto Show in October, 2003. It marked the return of the sporty front engine/rear drive configuration in a full-sized American sedan.

To address the needs of buyers that wanted a sporting American sedan but faced less than ideal weather for much of the year, Chrysler released the Hemi-powered AWD version of the 300C.

Chrysler uses an emblem that recalls the famous Letter Cars from the 1950s and early 1960s, yet it isn't a slavish retro piece. Since its introduction, the current 300C has been a popular vehicle in the American market.

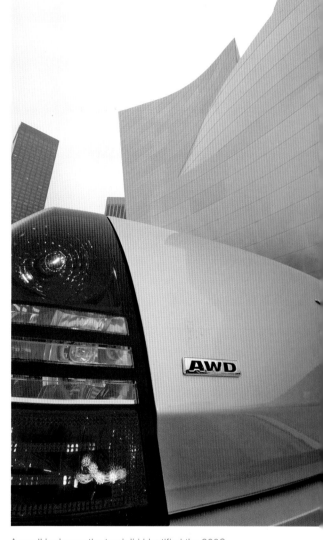

A small badge on the trunk lid identified the 300C AWD as a four-season full-sized sport sedan.

The 300C is a great car, but it's a luxury sedan and not a muscle car, so Dodge revived the Charger name for the 2006 model year. In Daytona R/T form, the car is powered by a 350-horsepower Hemi. This 345-cubic-inch pushrod V-8 matches its fabled 426-cubic-inch predecessor's SAE net horsepower rating, as well as the 390 lb-ft of torque (SAE net) that the older 426-cubic-inch version produced. And it does all this while still earning an EPA-estimated 25 miles per gallon, about five times as many miles per gallon as its legendary predecessor.

SRT8

Chrysler's old racing department never really went away. Even in the darkest days of the smog-motor era of the 1970s and early 1980s, a time when Chrysler Corporation was seeking government help to stay afloat, speed-crazed miscreants within the company could be found in some dark corner, plotting high-performance mischief. Such clandestine development led to cars like the Viper and the Prowler. The acronym for this group has morphed over the years, going from Specialty Vehicle Engineering (SVE) to Performance Vehicle Operations (PVO) to the current Street/Racing Technology (SRT). By whatever acronym they used, these people have always been the spiritual descendants of the hot rod boys and Ram Chargers who used to tear up Woodward Avenue back in the day. As could be expected, this group had its collective way with the new Hemi.

SRT models receive a number of exterior enhancements designed to improve both the looks of the vehicle and its performance. A deeper front air dam aids in the ability of the 300 SRT-8 to cleave the air in its rush to the horizon.

Serious components for a serious car. Brembo is an Italian maker of very high-performance brakes, and when Chrysler wanted to but top-shelf binders on the very fast SRT-8 line of vehicles, Brembo got the nod.

A small lip spoiler on the trunk lid of the 300 SRT-8 is a subtle touch, effective at managing airflow and a discrete styling statement. The huge tires are not as discrete.

Lurking beneath the attractive intake runners is a 6.1-liter normally aspirated Hemi that will churn out 425-horsepower all day. Docile at light throttle, it pulls like a locomotive when prodded.

Clear, easy-to-read instrumentation is important when there are 425 horses living on the other side of the firewall. Electronically limited to 155 miles per hour, the 300 SRT-8 is an example of having your high-performance in a livable package.

Chrysler kept the 300 SRT-8's visual drama low, with modest badging and subdued colors. The drama ratcheted up very quickly when the accelerator was slammed to the floor.

Vehicles with the Chrysler badge reside at the top of the Mopar pecking order, and a plush, comfortable interior is a matter of course. The 300 SRT8 is fully loaded; an ideal vehicle to dash across town or across country.

The coupling of the SRT division with the new Hemi engine resulted in the SRT8, a Hemi that produces 425 horsepower and 420 lb-ft of torque. This modern Hemi produces net ratings that equal the old engine's gross ratings. That's enough to propel the Charger through the quarter-mile in the 13-second bracket, despite the car's weighing a hefty 4,200 pounds.

continued on page 311

Time to grab a few postcards and hit the road! With its graceful roof line and rear hatch that opened well into the roof, accessing the luggage in a Dodge Magnum is a breeze.

Four letters that say so much. With cylinder de-activation, the 5.7-liter Hemi uses just four cylinders under light throttle—giving the engine respectable fuel economy numbers—but instantly accesses full power when needed.

Spacious and comfortably appointed, the Magnum R/T Hemi uses a tasteful two-tone interior motif to impart a sense of class and sportiness. The Hemi engine is only available with a Manu-Matic automatic transmission, but a slick shifter allows for full driver control.

Poised to dive into the traffic flow, a Magnum R/T Hemi wears elegant polished alloy wheels, reducing unsprung weight and improving handling. It doesn't hurt that they look great.

A vivid car needs a vivid setting. The Magnum R/T Hemi is one fast wagon, and it can run with the best available.

For wagon drivers who want to kick serious butt, the Magnum SRT-8 is the way to go—huge wheels, a lowered stance, and, when painted in a menacing color, it looked like it was ready for Darth Vader to climb in and take the wheel.

Long intake runners help the SRT-8 6.1-liter V-8 develop 425-horsepower, enough to propel the Magnum to 60 miles per hour in just five seconds and cover the quarter-mile in the 13 second range—on street tires!

Sourced from then-parent company Daimler, the slick shifter is the same seen in many Mercedes-Benz automobiles. That's a good thing with 425-horsepower at the other end of the shifter.

Dodge inserted a small SRT badge in the grille of the Magnum SRT-8, in case someone missed the lowered air dam and huge rolling stock.

Bright red Brembo calipers clamped down on the rotors of the Magnum SRT-8 effectively enough to provide fade-free braking time and again.

Dodge returned to its performance past with the installation of a 425-horsepower V-8 in a street car, but few expected to see the huge 6.1-liter engine in a station wagon.

As a people/cargo hauler, few vehicles can touch the Magnum.

Purists scoffed that a Charger could have four doors, but the public has embraced the Dodge version of the 300. Add an SRT-8 driveline, and the number of doors falls into insignificance.

Simple 20-inch five-spoke alloy wheels surround huge 14.2-inch front rotors, squeezed by fade-resistant Brembo calipers. Anti-Lock Brakes are standard.

continued from page 301

The SRT8 gets its extra horsepower honestly, through more cubic inches—the SRT8 displacement grew to 370 cubic inches (or 6.1 liters). The increased displacement comes via a bore that's increased to 4.05 inches. The cylinder block has a reinforced bulkhead to handle the extra loads generated by the larger pistons. The engine uses a relatively high compression ratio (10.3:1), and jets squirt oil at the underside of the pistons to help keep them cool. Like its predecessor, the 426 street Hemi, the SRT8 is loaded with high-grade performance parts. It has a billet-steel camshaft with more lift, longer duration, and more overlap than the cam in the smaller engine. Hollow stemmed intake valves measure 2.07 inches, versus 2 inches for the 345-cubic-inch engine, and the 1.59-inch exhaust valves are sodium-filled. Fuel enters the engine via a freer-flowing fuel injection system, and spent gasses exit via genuine tubular headers.

And like its predecessor, the new top-dog Hemi engine is expensive. All those good parts don't come cheap, whether those parts make up an old street Hemi or the new engine. A 2006 Charger Daytona R/T cost $35,794. The 2006 Charger SRT8 cost $43,730 (though, in all fairness, the SRT8 price included a $2,100 gas-guzzler tax).

continued on page 318

Subtle it ain't; the Charger SRT-8 is a speeding ticket waiting to happen. The long wheelbase and short overhangs mean a large interior and comfortable highway manners. The strong engine means considerable velocity on cue.

The large trunk-mounted wing was mostly for show, but it made identifying the Charger SRT-8 much easier than the small badge.

The huge hood scoop on the Charger SRT-8 is non-functional, but it gives the 4-door muscle sedan plenty of visual drama. The gunsight grille is a styling cue seen on all Dodge vehicles; it gives the Charger an aggressive front end.

This is one Jeep model that won't be challenging Moab, but for tackling the Interstate Highway system, the Grand Cherokee SRT-8, with its all-wheel-drive system, can handle almost anything Mother Nature can dish out.

No previous Jeep has enjoyed a 425-horsepower engine, and with 6.1-liters of grunt, the Grand Cherokee SRT-8 is probably the fastest Jeep in history. A brace connects the top of the front shock towers, increasing the vehicle's rigidity.

Despite it being a Jeep, the interior of the Grand Cherokee SRT-8 is upscale and well designed. Deeply bolstered seats hold the occupants in place during enthusiastic maneuvers.

Jeep affixed this badge onto the rear of the Grand Cherokee SRT-8 so other drivers would know what had just rocketed past them. With AWD, the powerful Jeep can be driven year-round in all kinds of conditions.

Embroidered emblems identify these sport seats as being fitted in an SRT-8 product, in this case the Grand Cherokee.

The Grand Cherokee SRT-8 uses a huge pair of
center-mounted exhaust tips to tickle the ear
under heavy throttle. Because the exhaust is
routed where a trailer hitch would normally be, this
performance vehicle can't be configured to tow
anything. But it hauls plenty.

continued from page 311

REBIRTH OF THE CHALLENGER

Everyone expected Dodge to bring back the Charger. What no one expected was that the new car would have four doors. In the past, all muscle cars have had two doors.

For those who refuse to accept a four-door muscle car, DaimlerChrysler developed a modern rendition of Dodge's original pony car, the Challenger. (There will be no new 'Cuda, since DaimlerChrysler—the temporary and unhappy company that formed when Daimler Benz bought Chrysler in the 1990s and dissolved when Daimler sold Chrysler to the investment group Cerebus in 2007—pulled the plug on the Plymouth brand after the 2001 model year.)

The new Challenger is larger than its illustrious ancestor. Its 116-inch wheelbase is 6 inches longer than that of the original 1970 E-body challenger (8 inches longer than Plymouth's Barracuda) and its overall length of 197.8 inches is almost 9 inches longer than the original car. (The new Challenger is over 11 inches longer than the original 'Cuda.) Even with larger

Designed by Michael Castiglione, the Dodge *Challenger Concept* vehicle uses the E-body as inspiration. The full-width grill and heavily-hooded headlights are pure period Challenger. Chrysler unveiled the car at the January 2006 North American International Auto Show in Detroit.

With its long hood/short deck proportions, the *Challenger Concept* is true to the original Pony Car formula. The kick-up on the rear quarter is a key stylistic element that evokes the 1970 Challenger. The overwhelmingly positive response to the *Challenger Concept* led Chrysler to build a production version.

The *Challenger Concept* used a carbon fiber hood with two stripes left unpainted, creating a dramatic graphic pattern. The production car makes due with a steel hood and faux carbon-fiber decals.

With the recessed grille and quad-headlights, the *Challenger Concept* has a dramatic front end. The traditional Dodge gunsight grille is in the area between the lights.

proportions, Dodge designers have done a commendable job recreating the classic E-body look in a car with modern aerodynamic efficiency. Perhaps the most visible differences are the shorter front and rear overhangs on the new car.

One area where the new Challenger pays faithful tribute to the original is in its engine bay. All the 2008 production models are equipped with the SRT8 Hemi. According to Dodge, the new Challenger turns in a 13-second-flat quarter-mile time and has a top speed of 174 miles per hour.

It took Metalcrafters six months to build the *Challenger Concept*. The white strips beneath the taillight assembly are back-up lights.

Beginning with the LX platform, the designers had to work with different window locations and a longer wheelbase than the original Challenger. The result is a car with a rich flavor of the E-body, but not a carbon copy.

From its full-width grille opening to its long hood/short deck proportions, the 2008 Challenger fits in well with muscle cars, old and new.

With the headlights pushed to the outside of the huge grill opening, and the turn signal/parking lamps just inboard, the front of the Challenger presents a dramatic look. The headlights are projector beams.

After a *Challenger Concept* drew rave reviews at the January 2006 North American International Auto Show in Detroit, announced it would build production versions. SRT8 examples began rolling off the assembly line in early 2008, all equipped with five-speed automatic transmissions, and production of standard 5.7-liter versions will begin for the 2009 model year. At that time Chrysler will offer a six-speed manual transmission with a classic Hurst-style pistol-grip shifter, a design that became a hallmark of Chrysler muscle cars from the 1970s. Chrysler capped total production at 6,400 SRT8 units for 2008. This relatively low production volume has led to price inflation at the dealer level. Reportedly, dealers were charging up to a 100 percent premium over the car's $37,995 base price for the first limited run of SRT8 Challengers. Given the dramatic appreciation of Hemi-powered E bodies from the classic muscle car era, it's a safe bet that many of these early production cars will live their lives in collections rather than out on the street.

The first Challenger SRT8—serial number one—was auctioned off at the Barrett-Jackson Collector Car Auction for $400,000 on January 18, 2008. This auction took place several weeks before the February 6, 2008, public unveiling of the production car at the Chicago Auto Show.

Dodge initially offered the Challenger in three colors: Hemi Orange, Silver, and Black. The latter packs a significant metallic content. With its 5-mph front bumper, the designers faced a challenge in trying to maintain the aggressive front-end profile of the 1970s-era cars, but they pulled it off well.

Another Challenger SRT8 bearing the serial number 43—Richard Petty's racing number—was auctioned on eBay on February 13, 2008, as part of the celebration of Petty Enterprises' 50th anniversary. As could be expected, that car was painted B5 Blue, otherwise know as "Petty Blue." Chrysler donated proceeds from both auctions to charity.

Faux hood scoops maintain a visual lineage to the original Challenger and provide some good real estate for mounting the engine callouts. The "carbon-fiber" hood section is actually an appliqué, meant to resemble the concept car's carbon fiber hood.

Full-width taillights and a center-mounted back-up light are pure 1970 Challenger. The rear spoiler looks like it was pulled straight off of a 1970 Challenger T/A.

When Chrysler affixes this badge to a vehicle, it's guaranteed to be an exciting ride. The SRT team has a long history of "enhancing" regular street vehicles into affordable thrill rides.

Chrysler built just 6,400 Challengers—all SRT8s—for the 2008 model year.

The Hemi Orange stripe on the SRT seats are a nice styling touch in an otherwise standard corporate interior. A wilder interior was planned, but at the eleventh hour cost concerns led designers to pursue a more conventional approach.

"426 CUBIC INCHES OF LEASHED FURY"

Just as had happened with the original Challenger, Chrysler introduced the 2008 version into an uncertain and changing marketplace. As was the case in 1970, America was slowly winding down from a long, unpopular war. And now as then, gas prices are climbing upward, with no indication they will stop anytime soon. Once again, safety Nazis are starting to proselytize about the wages of fast-car sin, and once again the government is instituting a new round of emissions regulations.

But if the interest in the car at the Barrett-Jackson Auction is any gauge, Chrysler should sell plenty of new Challengers. The new Hemi-powered cars are vastly improved over the old muscle cars in every conceivable way—quality control, efficiency, performance.

The Challenger SRT8's beefy 6.1-liter Hemi engine looks almost as great as it sounds. Long alloy intake runners not only dress up the engine compartment, but also help the 425-horsepower V-8 to breathe at high rpm.

Still, good as the new cars are, something keeps drawing us back to the old Hemis. It's something less concrete than noise levels and reliability ratings. In *Muscle Car Confidential* author Joe Oldham describes the visceral appeal of the 426 Hemi:

> As far as ambiance from the driver's seat, no amount of modern technology can match the sheer thrill of being the master of 426 cubic inches of unleashed fury. . . . There's no real way to describe in words the sound of eight Carter AFB barrels opening up on top of a 426-cubic-inch hemispherical combustion chamber

The 2008 Challenger SRT8 wears a fuel filler cap that looks like it was pulled directly from an early-70s-era Challenger. Weighing in at a total 4,140 pounds, and matched with an überpowered Hemi that simply begs to be flogged, drivers of this divine machine will be opening their filler caps rather frequently.

engine. But I'll try. It starts as a low moan, slowly rising into a wail that eventually turns into a shriek, a shriek that threatens to suck not only the surrounding air but also the hood itself and the closest two fenders directly into the shaker hood scoop.

As is often the case, Mr. Oldham gets right to the very core of the matter. All the aspects of its amazing history help account for the Hemi's mythological status—its racing provenance, its exclusivity, its rarity—but the Hemi experience—that sound, that feel, that brutal *presence*—is the reason the myth of the Hemi lives on stronger than ever. ■

INDEX

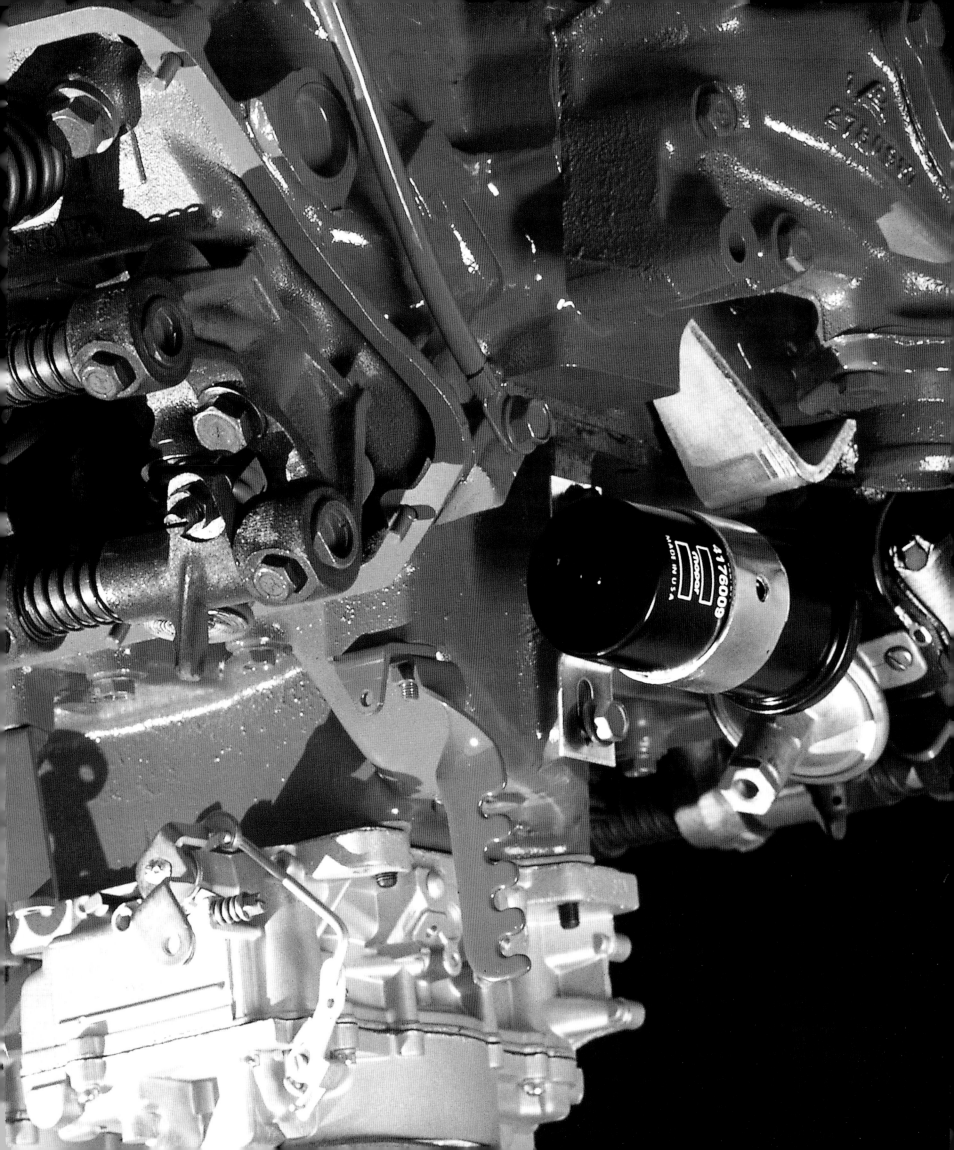